IVP PRAXIS
EQUIPPING LEADERS FOR MINISTRY

"...TO EQUIP HIS PEOPLE FOR WORKS OF SERVICE,
SO THAT THE BODY OF CHRIST MAY BE BUILT UP."

EPHESIANS 4:12

God has called us to ministry. But it's not enough to have a vision for ministry if you don't have the practical skills for it. Nor is it enough to do the work of ministry if what you do is headed in the wrong direction. We need both vision *and* expertise for effective ministry. We need *praxis*.

Praxis puts theory into practice. It brings cutting-edge ministry expertise from visionary practitioners. You'll find sound biblical and theological foundations for ministry in the real world, with concrete examples for effective action and pastoral ministry. Praxis books are more than the "how to" – they're also the "why to." And because *being* is every bit as important as *doing*, Praxis attends to the inner life of the leader as well as the outer work of ministry. Feed your soul, and feed your ministry.

If you are called to ministry, you know you can't do it on your own. Let Praxis provide the companions you need to equip God's people for life in the kingdom.

www.ivpress.com/praxis

LANCE FORD
& BRAD BRISCO

THE MISSIONAL QUEST

BECOMING A CHURCH OF THE LONG RUN

IVP Books

An imprint of InterVarsity Press
Downers Grove, Illinois

InterVarsity Press
P.O. Box 1400, Downers Grove, IL 60515-1426
World Wide Web: www.ivpress.com
Email: email@ivpress.com

InterVarsity Press® is the book-publishing division of InterVarsity Christian Fellowship/USA®, a movement of students and faculty active on campus at hundreds of universities, colleges and schools of nursing in the United States of America, and a member movement of the International Fellowship of Evangelical Students. For information about local and regional activities, write Public Relations Dept., InterVarsity Christian Fellowship/USA, 6400 Schroeder Rd., P.O. Box 7895, Madison, WI 53707-7895, or visit the IVCF website at www.intervarsity.org.

All Scripture quotations, unless otherwise indicated, are taken from THE HOLY BIBLE, NEW INTERNATIONAL VERSION®, NIV® Copyright © 1973, 1978, 1984, 2011 by Biblica, Inc.™ Used by permission. All rights reserved worldwide.

While all stories in this book are true, some names and identifying information in this book have been changed to protect the privacy of the individuals involved.

Figure 1.1 adapted from Drew Goodmanson's "triperspectival ecclesiology" as described in "The Decline of the Western Church and the Call to Renew Your Church's Ecclesiology," May 7, 2007, www.goodmanson.com/church/the-decline-of-the-western-church-and-the-call-to-renew-your-churchs-ecclesiology/.

Figure 3.1 adapted from Alan Roxburgh, Crossing the Bridge: Church Leadership in a Time of Change *(Rancho Santa Margarita, CA: Percept Group, 2000), p. 25.*

Figure 4.1 taken from Jay Pathak and Dave Runyon, The Art of Neighboring: Building Genuine Relationships Right Outside Your Door *(Grand Rapids: Baker, 2012), p. 38. Used by permission.*

Design: Cindy Kiple
Interior design: Beth Hagenberg
Images: rural chapel: © István Csák/iStockphoto
　　binoculars: © Evgeny Karandaev/iStockphoto

ISBN 978-0-8308-4105-9 (paper)
ISBN 978-0-8308-9578-6 (digital)

Printed in the United States of America ∞

Library of Congress Cataloging-in-Publication Data
A catalog record for this book is available from the Library of Congress.

P	18	17	16	15	14	13	12	11	10	9	8	7	6	5	4	3	2	1
Y	28	27	26	25	24	23	22	21	20	19	18	17	16	15	14	13		

From Lance
To my mother, Beth Ford.
Your contagious smile and sweet spirit has touched
everyone who has been on the sacred ground of your presence.
Thank you for showing me a lifetime of willingness to work hard,
laugh loud and love unconditionally.

From Brad
To my incredible wife, Mischele.
Thanks for pulling our family into engaging a segment of
God's mission that we would have never ventured into without
your consistent challenge and tireless leadership.

Contents

Foreword

*I*n an oft-quoted portion from the movie *The Princess Bride*, the frustrated Vizzini constantly shouts "Inconceivable!" His traveling companion Inigo Montoya eventually comments, "You keep using that word. I do not think it means what you think it means."

The popularity and prolific use of the word *missional* reminds me of this scene. When we begin to talk about "the mission of the triune God to glorify himself," what do we mean?

During the past half-century, there has been significant shift from understanding mission as simply the geographical expansion of the Christian faith from the West to the non-Christian world, toward a more expansive understanding of God's mission—particularly within a trinitarian theological framework. The *missio Dei*, a Latin phrase for the "sending of God" or the "mission of God," has become the milestone concept of the twentieth century's theology of mission. Today just about everyone believes in the *missio Dei* as an idea rooted in Scripture.

In short, *mission* refers to its fixed basis—the movement of the Father in sending his Son and Spirit. God is ontologically "missionary," and as God is the acting subject in his self-revelation, he maintains the initiative in this activity. We must start with the *missio Dei*.

This divine missionary activity includes yet another note-worthy shift in thought: the Father, Son and Holy Spirit sending the church into the world. Mission is God's work in the world; the church is an instrument for that mission. There is a church because there is a mission, not vice versa.

The mission of God calls us toward action. Christians, individually and corporately, are called to live pressing toward missional activity in the world.

My friends Lance Ford and Brad Brisco lay hold of this understanding and challenge in *The Missional Quest*. They succinctly explain how the church is created and designed to be on mission as its central purpose, not as an auxiliary arm or a program among many others. Both of these men are committed to encouraging the church to good works and to illustrating what it means for a church to be living as sent vehicle.

Lance and Brad expertly get the conversation about mission out of the weeds and onto the fairway, where the church will have a clear view of the direction with solid theological under-girding. Notable is their method of going beyond definitions and into practical applications churches and pastors can take to further their missional engagement and lifestyle. They illustrate the need for "everyday Christians to be on everyday mission" within the rhythms of the kingdom.

This "kingdom mentality" draws on the prevailing missionary text of John 20:21. Christ, in his own "sentness," commands the sending of the Christian community. *Missio Dei*, therefore, expresses this missionary existence of the Christian community. We are to live sent.

The New Testament undoubtedly places the mission of the church within the larger context of God's purpose to restore the whole creation (Rom 8:18-25; Col 1:20). But it also gives the church a focal occupation in the life of the kingdom: God's biblically mandated vessel for his redemptive agenda in the world.

Thus, the goal of the missional quest on which we find ourselves is the end-game described in the Scriptures—a redeemed people dwelling with God in a redeemed creation; a creation that will have experienced people of every tribe, tongue and nation responding in lifelong worship to King Jesus.

I'm thankful that my friends Brad and Lance point us to the ultimate goal of that missional quest.

Ed Stetzer

Introduction

Before the First Step

• • •

*The illiterate of the twenty-first century
will not be those who cannot read and write,
but those who cannot learn, unlearn, and relearn.*

ALVIN TOFFLER

Whether you have been on it for a while or this is your first venture into the missional conversation, welcome to the journey! While it is a road that many have been traveling for some time, others are just now getting their bearings and are beginning to discover why this is such an important topic for the church in North America. If you are fairly new to the discussion, a word of warning may be in order. Along the way you will experience times of frustration and bewilderment toward outdated and unbiblical ideas woven together with wonderful times of encouragement, discovery and adventure. Regardless of the bumps, however, you will discover this is one journey that must be taken.

If you are a veteran of the missional literature we hope you will find this book a resource that brings affirmation and additional clarity to your journey. Further we hope you discover *The Missional Quest* to be unique from other books in the missional genre in at least one way. We have written the book to provide very simple—but not always easy—steps to move an existing congregation in a missional direction.

Over the past several years we have worked with many dying and stagnant churches that have heard whispers from the missional dialogue. These churches' leaders may have read something from such authors as Alan Hirsch, Michael Frost, Hugh Halter, Neil Cole or others, but they just didn't know how to apply it in their local congregation. They knew there was profound truth in what was being written. They realized that the church growth methods on which their church was built were no longer sound or applicable. They acknowledged that there was a more theologically robust way of understanding mission and the church. And they knew their church must think differently about its place in the community and neighborhood.

But they wondered how to go about implementing the necessary change. What should be the first step? What church programs needed to be killed? And what new activities did the church need to engage? We believe this book will help you begin to answer those and many other questions you may be asking about leading your church on a missional quest.

The layout of the book is very intentional. The first section is titled "Fostering a Missional Mindset." And the first chapter is about how the church should think. It speaks to what we call the theological foundations. As a result of four decades of church growth thinking, most of us have deeply held assumptions about God, church and mission that must to be challenged or realigned.

Without such realignment, we run the risk of simply attaching the word *missional* onto everything we are already doing and ignoring the significant changes necessary. A genuine missional movement is not about tweaking the way we do church. Instead, it is a complete and thorough recalibration of the way we understand God's mission in the world and how we are to participate in it.

The hearts and minds of the people in our congregations must be captured by a revolutionary way of thinking about and living out the Christian life. And this simply will not happen if we don't begin the journey with serious theological reflection.

Before we ask what should we *do*—or what are the action steps—we must first ask *why?* Why does the religious landscape in America seem to be changing so quickly? Why don't the strategies and models for church growth from the past seem to "work" like they used to? And more importantly, why do we need to reconsider the nature and essence of the church? Why does the church in North America need to rethink mission? Why do we need to change the way we live our lives, individually and collectively as the body of Jesus? Addressing questions like these will prompt us to think both biblically and missiologically. We will begin to think like a missionary. Only today the mission field is not in a faraway land; it is in our own backyard.

The benefit to starting with theological reflection is that it is the only way to fully understand the practices we should be engaging. In other words, this must be a theological process and not just a pragmatic one. Without serious reflection on the missionary nature of the church, we will not completely grasp the fact that we are all missionaries sent into a local context. Without thinking well on the incarnation of Jesus, we will not totally comprehend the crucial posture of humility and sacrifice. Without seriously considering the doctrine of the *missio Dei*, we will not recognize the importance of discovery and discernment throughout our missionary engagement.

With this in mind, we simply encourage you not to move to the rest of the book too quickly. Make sure you understand the implications of each of these theological perspectives. Moreover, make certain the people in your congregation are fully aware of the importance and magnitude of these foundational pieces. Without a clear understanding, the changes we make will simply not be sustainable. People will question why the church has started doing certain things and stopped doing others. Without unlearning and relearning, there is no underlying rationale for change. However, we have discovered that when people are captivated by the missionary nature of God and the church and they realize that they were created as a sent missionary people, they are energized to be active participants in God's mission.

The second section of the book is titled "Fostering a Missional Posture (What Steps Are Necessary?)." In this portion of the book we take eight chapters to emphasize particular missionary principles and practices. Each of the chapters builds on the preceding chapter to create continuous momentum for equipping and releasing people into their local mission field. While we have made clear that we believe a rethinking of some core theological assumptions must take place, we also understand that we cannot simply think our way into a new way of acting. As important as chapter one is for moving a church in a missional direction, it is also true that people will never fully comprehend the concepts in the first chapter without stepping into mission as proposed in chapters two through nine. The good news is that as we struggle with the ideas from chapter one intellectually, at the same time we are engaging in mission in fresh new ways—and the learning curve for both increases significantly.

One additional aspect of the book that we hope you will find helpful are the sections we call "Steps on the Quest." Here we provide to church leaders practical suggestions for both communicating missional values and instilling core practices in a local congregation. There is no silver bullet for turning an inwardly focused, self-centered church into one that is fully engrossed in God's redemptive purposes. But we believe "Steps on the Quest" will give you specific and concrete ideas for moving in the right direction.

Alan Hirsch is well known for saying to the church in America, "We are perfectly designed to achieve what we are currently achieving." For anyone who has been paying close attention to the impact—or lack thereof—the church is having on the culture today, the achievement is clearly nothing to cheer about. The church must recapture its missionary identity and activate every Jesus-follower to engage wholeheartedly in the ongoing mission of God. Our hope is that this book will give you the practical tools to lead the church in getting the job done.

- Section One -

FOSTERING A MISSIONAL MINDSET

(How Should My Church Be Thinking?)

1

The Starting Line

Where the Missional Journey Begins

Brad Brisco

• • •

*Mission is not
primarily an activity of the church,
but an attribute of God.*

DAVID BOSCH

*If mission defines who Christ is,
and if Christ sends us as he was sent,
then mission defines who we are.*

ALBERT CURRY WINN

*The mission is God's.
The marvel is that God invites
us to join in.*

CHRISTOPHER WRIGHT

For nine years I taught a course on evangelism at a small Christian college. There was an exercise I would do every year to illustrate to the students just how inwardly focused most churches are. I would divide the whiteboard into two large columns. I asked the class to list all of the programs and ministries that their church had for those inside the church. In other words, activities just for church members. They would quickly create a very long list of things like Sunday morning worship, Sunday school, small groups, prayer groups, men's ministry, women's ministry, children's ministry, sports leagues, special fellowships—you get the picture. Occasionally a student might argue that some of the activities were open to those outside the church, but inevitably they agreed that each of the activities was tailored with church people in mind.

The next step was to list the ministries that their church had exclusively for those outside the church family. Beyond that, I would ask them to consider any training that the church provided for members to equip them to engage those outside the church. The contrast was striking. In more than one case a student couldn't name a single activity that his or her church had for those outside the church walls. All of the church's planning, finances and energy were spent exclusively on church members.

The vast majority of churches in America are not missional. But despite this reality, some people believe using the phrase "missional church" is redundant. "Of course the church is missional," they quip. The truth is that it should be redundant, but it isn't. The church in North America, generally speaking, is clearly not missional. Both individually and collectively, it simply does not consistently live out of its missional identity. So please don't say that missional church language is redundant. It is not.

So how are we to best understand the language of missional church? Unfortunately the word *missional* today seems to be connected to just about everything in the church world. Missional leadership. Missional evangelism. Missional youth ministry. Missional parenting. Missional denominations. Even missional clothing! Moreover, people are using the word *missional* to describe "new" ways to think about church growth, outreach, social justice and discipleship. Lance likes to refer to this crazy use of terminology as "applying missional paint." Buy a can of missional paint and brush it on to whatever the church is already doing. Just like that, it's missional!

But if we reject this overuse, what then does the word *missional* mean? Moving forward, how are we to best understand it? I usually respond by saying that I have a short answer and a long answer to this question.

The short answer is that missional is simply the adjective form of the noun *missionary*. Therefore when we use the language of "missional church," the word *missional* is used to describe the church as a missionary entity. The church doesn't just send missionaries, the church is the missionary.

Now for the long answer. When considering a more theologically rooted definition of the word *missional* we need to examine three chief distinc-

> **The church doesn't just send missionaries, the church is the missionary.**

tions. These are the theological foundations of a missional approach, which we believe must serve as the starting line to our journey. Each point deliberately confronts long-held assumptions most Christians have about God, the church and mission. Without serious attention to each of these three points, the missional journey will inevitably end prematurely.

THE MISSIONARY NATURE OF GOD AND THE CHURCH

The first shift in thinking that must take place relates to our understanding of the missionary nature of God and the church. When we think of the attributes of God, we most often think of characteristics such as holiness, sovereignty, wisdom, justice, love and so on. Rarely do we think of God's missionary nature. But Scripture teaches that God is a missionary God—a sending God.

What's more, the Bible is a missionary book. Scripture is generated by and is all about God's mission activity. The word *mission* is derived from the Latin *missio*, meaning "sending." And it is the central theme describing God's activity throughout all of history to restore creation. While often overlooked, one remarkable illustration in Scripture of God's missionary nature is found in the "sending language" that is prominent throughout the Bible.

From God's sending of Abram in Genesis 12 to the sending of his angel in Revelation 22, there are literally hundreds of examples that portray God as a missionary, sending God. In the Old Testament God is presented as the sovereign Lord who sends in order to express and complete his redemptive mission. The Hebrew verb "to send," *shelach*, is found nearly eight hundred times. While it is most often used in a variety of non-theological sayings and phrases,[1] it is employed more than two hundred times with God as the subject of the verb.[2] In other words, it is God who commissions and it is God who sends.

In the book of Exodus there is a fascinating dialogue surrounding God's prompting of Moses to confront Pharaoh. God is sending Moses to convince the king of Egypt to release the Israelites from bondage. In just six verses there are five references to sending. The Lord says:

"So now, go. I am *sending* you to Pharaoh to bring my people the Israelites out of Egypt."

But Moses said to God, "Who am I that I should go to Pharaoh and bring the Israelites out of Egypt?"

And God said, "I will be with you. And this will be the sign to you that it is I who have *sent* you: When you have brought the people out of Egypt, you will worship God on this mountain."

Moses said to God, "Suppose I go to the Israelites and say to them, 'The God of your fathers has *sent* me to you,' and they ask me, 'What is his name?' Then what shall I tell them?"

God said to Moses, "I AM WHO I AM. This is what you are to say to the Israelites: 'I AM has *sent* me to you.'"

God also said to Moses, "Say to the Israelites, 'The Lord, the God of your fathers—the God of Abraham, the God of Isaac and the God of Jacob—has *sent* me to you.'" (Ex 3:10-15, emphasis added)

The prominence of sending language is not only seen in the books of Genesis and Exodus; throughout all of the historical books God is a sending God. Throughout the poetic books God is a sending God. Throughout the prophetic books God is a sending God. When you consider the books of prophecy in the Old Testament, it is easy to see that the prophets were first and foremost people sent by God.

Perhaps the most dramatic illustration of sending in the Old Testament is found in Isaiah 6. In this passage we catch a glimpse of God's sending nature: "Then I heard the voice of the Lord saying, 'Whom shall I *send*? And who will go for us?'" To this Isaiah responds, "Here am I! Send *me*!" (Is 6:8, emphasis added).

Further, in the prophetic books it is interesting to note that the Old Testament ends with God promising through the words of the prophet Malachi to send a special messenger as the fore-runner of the Messiah: "I will send my messenger" (Mal 3:1). Then the New Testament begins with the arrival of that messenger in the person of John the Baptist, described in the Gospels as a man sent by God (Jn 1:6).

In the New Testament, sending language is found not only in the Gospels but also throughout the book of Acts and each of the Epistles. The most comprehensive collection of sending language, however, is found in the Gospel of John, where the word *send* or *sent* is used nearly sixty times. The majority of uses refers to the title of God as "one who sends" and of Jesus as the "one who is sent." All the way through John's Gospel we see God the Father sending the Son. God the Father and the Son sending the Spirit. And God the Father, Son and Spirit sending the church. In the final climactic sending passage in John's Gospel, Jesus makes clear that he is not only sent by the Father, but now he is the sender, as he sends the disciples: "As the Father has sent me, I am sending you" (Jn 20:21).

With this sentence Jesus is doing much more than drawing a vague parallel between his mission and ours. Deliberately and precisely he is making his mission the model for ours. Our understanding of the church's mission must flow from our understanding of Jesus' mission as reflected in the Gospels. Geoffrey Harris states it this way:

> The Gospels reflect the fact that mission is the essence of the Church's life and not just an aspect of it. The life of Jesus is invariably represented as being enacted in the world at large (and not in religious settings), among ordinary people of all sorts (and not just among believers) and, in particular, as reaching out to those beyond the normal scope and influence of the religious establishment. Jesus' early nickname,

"friend of sinners," is transformed in the Gospels from a term of abuse into a badge of honour and respect.[3]

The sending language in Scripture not only emphasizes the missionary nature of God, but it also stresses the importance of understanding the church as a sent, missionary body. God is a missionary God who sends a missionary church. As Jesus was sent into the world, we too are sent into the world.

At the core of the missional conversation is the idea that a genuine missional posture is a sending rather than an attractional one. Our friend Linda Burgquist likes to point out

God is a missionary God who sends a missionary church.

that Jesus did not assign the seventy to become a core group that would function as a new "come-to" structure; he instead sent them out by twos to engage the surrounding towns and villages. Likewise, we should be sending the people in the church out among the people of the world rather than attempting to attract the people of the world in among the people of the church. This is a crucial distinction because most people in the church today do not think of their congregation in a sending, missionary manner.

In the book *Missional Essentials* we highlight the two most prominent ways people today understand church.[4] The first view is what some call the "Reformation heritage" perspective.[5] The point is that Protestants have inherited a particular view of church from the Reformers, which emphasizes the right preaching of the Word, the right administration of the ordinances and the proper exercise of church discipline. This view has left us with an understanding of the church as a place where certain things happen—a person goes to church to hear the Bible taught "correctly," to participate in the Lord's Supper and baptism and, in some cases, to experience church discipline.

The second view is a slight variation on the "place where . . ." definition of the church. This "contemporary variation" view is perhaps the most prevalent way people in America understand the church today—that it is a vendor of religious goods and services. From this perspective, members are viewed as customers for whom religious goods and services are produced. Churchgoers expect the church to provide a wide range of religious services, such as great worship music, preaching, children's programs, small groups, parenting seminars and so on. If you are not convinced that this is the prevailing vision that most churches operate from, read the words of George Hunsberger as he critiques the church built on this foundation:

> Most of us value the use of many businesslike techniques and procedures in the life of the church but would be aghast at the suggestion that we fundamentally operate out of a model of the church as a business, a vendor of religious services. But consider the unconscious and unquestioned form of many of our carefully worded mission statements. It is amazing how many are cast something like this: "The mission of Anytown Community Church is to nurture its members in Christian faith and equip them for service and witness to Christ in the world." What follows tends to detail the educational, worship, witness, and justice commitments of the church. But notice how the text reads. The mission of this *church* is to nurture its *members*. . . . The members are not conceived, in such a statement, as *being* the church and themselves *having* a mission on which they have been collectively sent. Instead, they are the customers, the regular consumers for whom the religious services and goods produced by the "church" are intended.[6]

One of the major issues with both of these views of defining the church is that the church is seen as an institution that exists for the benefit of its members. Or, as Hunsberger states above, many people believe the mission of the church is to "nurture its members." But that is not the essence of the church! In fact, it is the exact opposite. In the words of Archbishop William Temple, the church is the only organization that exists for the sake of its nonmembers.

The alternative vision of the church is to see it as a people called and sent by God to participate in his redemptive mission for the world. The nature of the church—rooted in the very nature of God—is missionary. As William McAlpine puts it, "Rather than seeing ourselves primarily as a sending body, we must see ourselves as a body that is sent."[7] The church still gathers, but the difference is that we gather not for our own sake but for the sake of others. Or better yet, for the sake of God's mission. We come together regularly as a collective body to be equipped through teaching, prayer, worship and study, and then to be sent out into the world. The church is both a gathered and scattered people.

STEPS ON THE QUEST

Create opportunities to teach on the missionary nature of God. Highlight the missionary, sending language of Scripture on Sunday mornings and in small groups. Prominent sending passages include Genesis 12:1-3; Isaiah 6:1-9; 61:1-3; John 17:18; 20:21. Also refer to the appendix for a complete survey of sending language in John's Gospel.

INCARNATIONAL MISSION VERSUS EXTRACTIONAL MINISTRY

While the first theological distinction deals with the missionary nature of God and the "sentness" of the church, the second key concept has to do with how and where we are sent. The language of "incarnational mission" represents the embedding of our lives and the gospel into a local context. If the essence of missional living is sending, then the heart of incarnational mission is staying.

The heart of incarnational mission is staying.

The word *incarnation* comes from a Latin word that literally means "in the flesh." It refers to the act whereby God took it upon himself to enter into the depths of our world so that the reconciliation between himself and humanity could be brought about. The incarnation is God's ultimate missional participation in creation (Jn 3:16-17). When God entered into our world in and through the person of Jesus, he came to live among us (*eskenosen*—literally, "set up a tent"): "The Word became flesh and blood, and moved into the neighborhood" (Jn 1:14 *The Message*).

As Alan Hirsch writes, "The Incarnation not only qualifies God's acts in the world, but must also qualify ours. If God's central way of reaching his world was to incarnate himself in Jesus, then our way of reaching the world should likewise be incarnational."[8] However, not everyone believes that the incarnation should serve as a model for mission. Some believe that the phrase "incarnational mission" is misleading or even dangerous. They are afraid that the use of such language will diminish the theological integrity of the incarnation of Christ.

Acknowledging these concerns, we should note that there is absolutely no doubt that the incarnation of Jesus was a special, unrepeatable event. As we enter into the world of others, we certainly cannot take on another's identity in the way that Jesus did. He literally became one of us. Jesus was fully incarnated, taking on human flesh to rescue us from sin and death. But having said that, surely we can make a distinction between the incarnation and incarnational mission. As theologian Darrell Guder states, there may be a risk, but it is one clearly worth taking:

> Just as any theological concept is susceptible to distortion, there are ways of misconstruing the linkage of Christian mission with the incarnation. It is possible to dilute the uniqueness and centrality of the life, death, and resurrection of Jesus Christ when his incarnation becomes a model for Christian behavior. A primary ethical or moralistic interpretation of the life of Jesus, such as was characteristic of nineteenth-century liberal theology, often downplays or dilutes the event-character of the gospel.
>
> But it is that event character, the historical "happenedness" of Jesus' life that both enables and defines Christian witness. As we seek to explore the missional significance of the incarnation, we need to resist every temptation to dilute the centrality of the incarnation event. The risk represented by the concept of incarnational mission is worth taking, I think, especially as we are challenged to develop a viable mission theology for the Western world, which by common consent is now a very challenging mission field.[9]

There is much more that could be said concerning the use of incarnational language as a way to frame our understanding of mission. However, because there are several good resources that deal with the topic,[10] we want to move to the practical implications for existing congregations. If the incarnation provides a helpful way to understand how we should engage our local setting, then in what ways does this incarnational approach integrate with the principles of the church growth movement that has so greatly influenced the church in America over the past several decades?

Much of the discussion over the past several years has pitted two camps against one another. There are those in the missional-incarnational camp and those in the attractional, seeker-sensitive camp. But is it really an "either-or" discussion? Is there no room in our understanding of church and mission to see a "both-and" way of engaging our communities?

We have found the following diagram to be helpful in illustrating the necessity of a "both-and" approach to expressions of ecclesia—or church life.

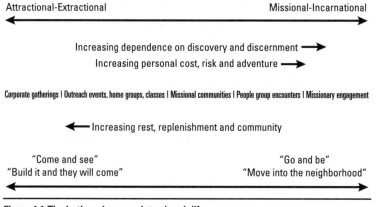

Figure 1.1. The both-and approach to church life

Although it is certainly not comprehensive, there are at least five different expressions of ecclesia that can be placed on a continuum. Those expressions toward the left side of the continuum are more attractional in nature, while those on the right side take on a much more missional-incarnational posture.

Now before we consider a description of each of the different expressions, a clarification of terminology may be necessary.

When we use the word *attractional* we are speaking of an approach to church that pours a disproportionate amount of time and resources into the corporate worship service to create a place that nonbelievers will want to come to and be exposed to the truth of Jesus. As discussed earlier, the church takes on the role of a vendor of religious goods and services.

Further, the term *attractional* describes our missionary stance in relation to our context. In other words, when we operate from an attractional paradigm, we are asking those outside the church to come to us rather than seeing ourselves as the missionary people of God who are sent to others. We are asking them to scale the cultural barriers that lie between where they live and where the church exists. In a very real sense, we are asking those outside the church to become the missionaries.

Now please do not confuse being attractional with being attractive. Our lives ought to be attractive to those around us because of what Jesus is doing in and through us. We should live lives that are alluring to others. People should be drawn to the church because it is made up of people whose lives are counterintuitive to the normal ways of the world. They are attractive because their lives exude grace, mercy, justice and wisdom.

This bit of confusion has led some to use the term *extractional* rather than *attractional*.[11] Extractional refers to the way the church has historically extracted new believers from their local context. When someone comes to Christ, the church is notorious for quickly removing them from their relational connections to attend a church service and inadvertently teaching them that "church is something they go to rather than who they are in the places they inhabit. So the church pulls them out of the contexts in which they live and often disconnects their contribution from their everyday context."[12] This is what is meant by the term "attractional-extractional" to describe the far left end of the continuum.

The far right of the continuum is illustrated by the missional-incarnational posture. Missional speaks to our direction—we are sent—while incarnational speaks to the manner in which we are sent. Incarnational mission must involve living in proximity with others. We simply "cannot demonstrate Christlikeness at a distance from those whom we feel called to serve."[13] Just as Jesus took on flesh and blood and moved into the neighborhood, we must do likewise. This may require moving geographically to be closer to those to whom God has sent us. At the very least it will demand creating time and space to be directly and actively involved in the lives of people we are seeking to reach.

In addition to the idea of proximity, incarnational mission also involves the idea of presence. Presence moves beyond proximity to identification and surrender. Jesus identified with and advocated for those he was called to. As Philippians 2 makes clear, Jesus humbled himself. He literally emptied himself for the sake of others. This realization suggests an incarnational approach that calls us to relational identification with our neighbors that will lead to tangible acts of love and sacrifice.

Moreover, when considering the significance of an incarnational paradigm it is helpful to recognize that Jesus' words from John 20:21, "As the Father has sent me, I am sending you," are most often used to emphasize the sending of the disciples and subsequently the church. But we must not neglect the first half of the passage. Jesus says, "As the Father has sent me." The word translated "as" (or in some translations "just as") means "like" or "in a similar manner."[14] In other words, we need to be sent like Jesus was sent. To whom and in what manner was Jesus sent? He was sent to the down-and-outers of society. He was with and for tax collectors, the oppressed, the poor and the diseased. Again, taking Jesus as our example, we are called to do likewise. R. Geoffrey Harris puts it this way:

> In an incarnational model of mission, those who join with Jesus are those who reach out to the marginalized. They do not simply offer "spiritual" salvation—forgiveness of sin or experience of God—but associate themselves with those most in need of a friend—with the Christ who asks a loose woman for water, and speaks at length to her; who is on the side of the woman taken in adultery, and stays to talk to her. The incarnate Christ is the one who sweats and agonizes with the little ones of the earth, who bleeds for those who are victims of corruption and the brutal misuse of power. Those who follow such a Christ in the world are in solidarity with those he most obviously came to help—not the righteous, but the lost.[15]

Now that we've clarified the terminology of the two poles on the continuum, let's consider five groupings that represent different forms and functions through which the church can express its identity.

Corporate gatherings. This would include weekly worship services as well as other larger gatherings where several smaller groups meet collectively for worship, teaching, prayer, fellowship and so on. Corporate gatherings for most churches are the clearest example of an attractional mindset. The church believes that if they provide high-quality programing in areas such as teaching, worship and children's ministry, people will be "attracted" to attend.

Outreach events, home groups, classes. This would include events such as block parties that take place on church property or in neighborhoods surrounding the church facility. This would also include other one-time outreach events such as concerts or plays. Other examples of outreach activities would include sports leagues, AWANA, vacation Bible school and so on.

Home groups are more traditional small groups or Bible studies organized around the need for greater community and discipleship for church members. Classes offered by the church would include topics addressing specific needs of the surrounding community. For example, a church may offer a marriage enrichment seminar or expertise on parenting.

While each of the examples from this expression of church involves some engagement outside the church walls—to conduct a class that is helpful you have to discover what the needs of the community are, for example—they still tend to lean more heavily on an attractional mindset. People still need to be persuaded to participate in what the church is offering.

Missional communities. The difference between a typical small group and a missional community is that most small groups are centered on the need to develop relationships. In fact, it can be argued that small group ministries were popularized decades ago by the need to "close the back door" of churches that were experiencing significant growth through the Sunday gathering but losing potential members just as quickly because these newcomers were not connecting with others in the church. Small groups became the primary way to assimilate people into the life of the church.

Also, traditional small groups attempt to focus on discipleship in the midst of group life. Most small groups engage in some type of Bible study or group curriculum. While one can certainly make the case that Bible study does not automatically lead to making disciples, for most small group ministries discipleship is at least the intent.

For missional communities, on the other hand, the starting

point is mission. Missional communities are catalyzed by and organized around mission. Relational community is still cultivated and discipleship remains a top priority, but both happen (we believe best) in, through and around missional engagement. While we will discuss the topic of missional communities much more in chapter seven, the point for now is to recognize what differentiates them from typical groups in most churches.

People group encounters. These can involve a wide range of missional activities that involve identifying and engaging certain affinity groups. For example, there are many "tribes" formed around hobbies or special interests such as art, music or sports. A church might identify ways they can partner with a local group of artists, form a team to join a sports league or lean relationally into a group of civic leaders.

People groups can also include those who share a common geographical or vocational connection. A church might "adopt" teachers from a school in the local community. Some churches have come alongside school athletic programs, especially in impoverished areas of the community, to provide proper sports gear and pregame meals.

In today's mobile environment people group encounters will certainly involve engaging a community's ethnic diversity. Nearly every city in the United States has pockets of ethnic groups made up of recent immigrants to the country as well as second and third generations that have grown up here. Each group provides unique cultural challenges in terms of relating to a local church.

Regardless of the type or size of the group, a missional-incarnational approach will prompt us to ask what it looks like to incarnate the gospel in this particular place, at this particular time, to this particular people group.

Missionary engagement. This last category addresses individual missionary activity. You will never have a missional church without missional people who engage the lives of others where they live, where they work and where they play. In other words, every church member must see him- or herself as a missionary living out their missional calling in their neighborhood, through their vocation and in social settings (third places) within the local community. We will speak much more on each of these topics in chapters four through six.

Now imagine three arrows running from one end of the continuum to the other. The first arrow goes from the "corporate worship" category (on the attractional end of the continuum) to "missionary engagement" on the missional-incarnational end of the spectrum. This arrow represents the necessity of increasing dependence on discovery and discernment toward God's activity. As we move in a missional-incarnational direction we must experience a heightened sensitivity to where and how God's Spirit is moving.

Please do not hear what we are not saying. This does not mean that more attractional expressions of church are somehow void of God's activity. We should be listening closely to God's leading in every aspect of the life of the church. We are simply saying that as we move into areas that are less familiar, perhaps more "risky," we will need to be more spiritually aware of our surroundings and how God is moving in the lives of the people there.

The troubling reality is that we have all seen too many cases where large gatherings are more about human ingenuity than about reliance on the Spirit. That simply cannot be the case when we are living out missionality in a local setting. We must rely on the Spirit to know when, where and how to participate in what the Spirit is already doing in the places we inhabit. Further, we will have neither the passion nor the strength to live out an incarnational posture—for the sake of others—if we are not continually refreshed by the Spirit. We will expand on this topic in chapter two.

The second arrow points in the same direction as the first, but it illustrates the increasing personal cost, risk and adventure associated with a missional-incarnational stance. As we move into the expressions of church toward the right of the continuum, the costs in our lives will undoubtedly increase. For most people the only "cost" associated with the majority of church meetings is mere attendance, simply taking the time to be there when the gathered church meets. However, living for and with those God has sent us to will involve much greater commitments of both our time and resources. The more closely we follow Jesus into the hard places, the more sacrificial our lives must become (Lk 9:23).

In addition to increased personal cost, moving into relational proximity with others will encompass risk. People are messy. And the closer we lean into the lives of those around us, the messier things will become. The further we step beyond the safety of the Christian bubble, the greater the risk we encounter.

However, we must also acknowledge that in the midst of missionary engagement we experience the greatest opportunities for adventure. On the fringes of missionary activity we have the best vantage point to see what God is doing. When we are personally engaged in God's mission we experience firsthand how God is working. Therefore, this arrow highlights the necessity to move people from a passive, consumerist church mindset to missional engagement that involves both costs and great rewards.

The final arrow moves in the opposite direction. It starts on the right side of the continuum with "missionary engagement" and extends to "corporate worship" on the attractional side. This arrow represents the increasing opportunities for rest and replenishment that are available as we participate in local faith communities. It emphasizes the need for all expressions of the church. There are times, especially in seasons of intense missionary engagement, that we need to be able to gather with other believers to be refreshed through worship, study, prayer and community.

Now that we've considered each category, let's address why it is important to frame the apparent tension between an attractional approach on the one end and a missional-incarnational position on the other. There are at least three significant observations to underscore.

First, the issue of missional-incarnational vs. attractional is not an "either-or" proposition. The central issue is where is the emphasis in the life of the church. If the majority of the church's resources are spent on creating an environment to attract people to church activities, it will be extremely difficult to equip and release people in the church to engage missionally. This consumerist mindset develops when the programming of the church is seen to exist primarily for the use of church members. When people are attracted to the church because it is a vendor of religious goods and services, it is nearly impossible to move them to become sacrificial, "for-the-sake-of-others" missionaries. What you win people with is what you win them to.

Let's be clear: there is nothing wrong with attracting people to attend various meetings or activities of the church. The problem arises when it becomes the primary focus of the church. As a result the church will most likely miss what God is doing in the community around it. We will address this topic more fully in chapter three.

When evaluating church "success," we must move away from measuring numbers related to the large gathering. The traditional matrix of buildings, budgets and butts will no longer suffice. Instead the church must begin highlighting activities in the quadrants of missional communities, people group encounters and individual missionary engagement. New scorecards must be created in these areas to provide a better picture of how the church is engaging its community. We will address the need for developing new measurables in chapter nine.

When starting a new church, we must begin with missionary activity and not with the corporate gathering. Church planting over the past several decades has really been about planting a church service. Church planters have been encouraged to focus on the "launch," which is code for Sunday morning worship service. As already noted, when the emphasis is on the large gathering, we by default lose focus on what God is doing in the surrounding context.

Furthermore, because people today are less and less interested in the programs and activities of the church, starting a church by attempting to attract people to attend the corporate gathering is proving to be increasingly futile. On the other hand, when starting a new church by instilling a missional-incarnational DNA from the very beginning, the church can grow into other expressions of church life over time or, at the very least, at the same time.

A wonderful picture of this "both-and" mentality is illustrated in the life of New City Church, a church plant in a suburb of Kansas City. Within just six months of starting its first Sunday morning worship service the church had over three hundred attending its corporate gatherings. However, the rapid growth in Sunday services was not because of some great attractional strategy. Instead it was the result of the core group immersing themselves into the life of the surrounding community.

New City had planned twenty-five community outreach events prior to launching its Sunday service. Initially the purpose of these events was to raise awareness of the new church. However, as the church began to lean into the community through its various outreach activities, the needs of the people in the community began to capture the hearts of the church. As a result the church decided to push the launching of public worship services back to create more time to build relationships in the community. Matt Miller, pastor of New City, regularly reminds people that the weekend gathering is a time one day a week to celebrate how the church is serving the neighborhood every day of the week.

New City is a great example of how a church can be engaged in mission in every expression of church life. It has equipped and released dozens of "missionaries" into the surrounding neighborhoods. It has adopted various people groups in the community. It has started missional communities that each have their own mission focus. And it provides training in the church facility to address specific community needs.

Perhaps the best example of the "both-and" mentality of New City's engagement can be seen in its relationship with an elementary school that is literally a few feet out the back door of the church's meeting space. This particular school is what is referred to as a Title One school, meaning that nearly all of the students receive free or reduced-price lunches. The school district refers to the school as an urban school in a suburban setting. The vast majority of the students walk to school from the surrounding apartment complexes. The school as a whole and the students in particular are under constant financial strain. Families in the neighborhood that have the financial means to do so choose to homeschool, send their kids to private school or transfer to another elementary school outside the area.

After discovering these needs and discerning how God was

leading the church to be involved, New City decided to do all they could to bless the school. They "adopted" every teacher in the school and found dozens of ways to be a blessing to every student. And as the students captured the hearts of the church, the church's involvement began to move beyond activities. Church families began moving into the community so their kids could be a part of the school. While others were moving out, New City was moving in.

Individual families and the church body as a whole discovered ways to engage every aspect of the life of the school. Here's a wonderful example of just how important New City has become to the life and vitality of the school: After just six months, the school presented Matt with a "lifetime achievement award" for assisting the school in fulfilling its purpose in the lives of the students.

One final example that illustrates how the people of New City have incarnated their lives into the lives of students involves another staff member named Chris Moix. Chris was disposing of several bags of trash in the dumpster behind the church on the last day of school. Because it was during recess a few of the students noticed Chris through the chainlink fence. The students began bringing their school yearbooks to the fence to have Chris sign their books. As students began to come to the fence with books and pens in hand, more students began to gather to request a signature. As Chris signed one book and handed it over the fence, another student would ask him to sign his or her book. For several minutes there was a constant exchanging of books, until everyone got Chris's signature. Chris said he felt like a rock star.

When Chris first told me this story, I wanted to cry. Chris and the church had come to mean so much to these elementary kids that they wanted his signature. And all of this took place not because New City has a great Sunday morning gathering but because the people of New City understand that they are the sent, missionary people of God.

STEPS ON THE QUEST

Take an assessment. In what categories of the diagram do the majority of your church's programs currently fall? What would it take to cultivate movement toward the other expressions of church? Create an opportunity to share the diagram with others in the church. What ideas do they have for other expressions of church?

PARTICIPATING IN THE *MISSIO DEI*

The third key theological foundation involves the concept of the *missio Dei*, or "mission of God." It is God who has a mission to set things right in a broken world—to redeem and restore it to what was always intended. Therefore mission is not a program of the church. It is not something we invent. Mission is not something we initiate. Instead mission flows directly from the nature and purposes of a missionary God. It is not that the church has a mission; it is that God's mission has a church. In other words, it is God's mission, and the church is an instrument created by God to be sent into the world to join in his mission. This is a complete game-changer in at least two ways.

It is not that the church has a mission; it is that God's mission has a church.

First, a *missio Dei* perspective should challenge the church to rethink mission. Most congregations view missions as one activity among many other equally important functions of the church. Therefore, the missions program is seen alongside that of worship, small groups, women's ministries, youth and children's ministries, and so on. When a church views missions in this way, the job of the missions committee is to determine where the missions budget should be spent rather than seeing that everything the church does is informed by God's mission.

When the church begins to define itself as an agent of God's mission, it will begin to organize every activity of the church around the *missio Dei*. Mission becomes the organizing principle, which means that mission goes beyond being some sort of optional activity for the church. Instead God's mission is seen as "the organizing axis of the church. The life of the church revolves around it. This is not to say that we don't do corporate worship, develop community, and make disciples, but that these are catalyzed by and organized around the mission function. Only in this way can we be truly missional. Merely adding serving events or special outreach days to our church schedules will not develop missional people nor make a missional church."[16]

STEPS ON THE QUEST

Begin asking how certain programs or activities of your church would change if informed by God's mission. How might small groups operate differently if shaped by God's mission? How would the corporate teaching of Scripture be different? How might worship change?

Determining where and how we engage in God's mission is the second way a *missio Dei* theology influences our activity. If the mission is God's—and it is—then how do we step into it?

How do we truly participate in what God is doing? Author Geoffrey Harris provides these helpful words:

> The average church member may be reassured to know that mission is instigated by the simple act of praying, and of listening to God, and following God's guidance. In such fundamental activities all Christians can participate. In addition, it is reassuring to know that God's Spirit is at work in the world prior to our engagement in any relationship or any work of mission. The presence of God in the world means that anyone embarking upon God's mission already has an ally and accomplice in the work. It becomes "mission alongside" rather than mission alone.[17]

In a small group curriculum titled *Missional Essentials*, I shared what I call the four Ds of missional engagement. It was my attempt to give practical handles to the kind of thinking shared in Harris's words above. If it is about God's mission and not ours, then how do we know where, when and how to participate in what God is doing?

Discover. The first step is to listen. Individually and collectively we must cultivate our ability to listen well on three fronts—to God, to the local community and to each other. It is simply impossible to ascertain the movement of God without carving out significant time to listen to his voice through prayer and Scripture as well as the voices of those we desire to serve. The first question we ask: Where is God actively at work in my community?

Discern. In addition to listening, participating in God's mission involves the difficult task of discernment. Not only will we need to discern what God is already doing, but we will also need to ask a follow-up question: "In light of my (our) gifts and resources, how does God want me to participate in what he is doing?" The fact is we can't do it all, which is true for both individual followers of Jesus and local congregations. But it is also true that God has gifted us all to do something! The point of discernment is to determine where and how to participate in God's mission.

Do. This may seem obvious, but the process of discernment is useless if we do not obey what God is calling us to do. When God prompts us to participate in what **The point of discernment is to determine where and how to participate in God's mission.**
he is doing in the lives of others, we must be obedient to respond.

Debrief. Throughout the process of engaging God's mission we must create opportunities to reflect on our missional involvement. Sometimes this simply means we need individual down time to reflect on our activities. We may need to ask God to affirm our involvement or to ask for clarity of direction. But it will also involve carving out time to reflect with others in our faith community. We need to hear what others are seeing and sensing concerning God's activities and to hear the stories of how others are engaging God's mission.

The four Ds help to put the emphasis on the place God has sent us and on how God has already been working in that place long before we ever arrived. The starting point must involve an attitude of listening and learning. Mark Van Steenwyk offers this added encouragement:

> Don't start doing things until you understand the ethos of the neighborhood. Let the spirit of the place make its impression. Fall in love with the little things. Get to know the people. If you start "doing your thing" before you are familiar with the place, then you're forcing things too much. Ministry should fit with how God is already working

in a place. If you start pushing your agenda before you start making friends with the neighbors and finding out about their lives, then you're a salesman, not a minister of reconciliation. And throughout it all, pray. Pray for spiritual eyesight. It is the Spirit's job to reveal Christ . . . not just to "them" but also to "you." Pray that you can see Christ's fingerprints in your neighborhood. Pray to see the face of Christ in the face of those who live around you. Pray for the Spirit to show you what is wrong in your area, and also what is right. Seek to understand.[18]

This chapter has been about laying the proper theological foundation for the missional conversation—or perhaps the missional conversion. For many in the church there is a conversion of thought and practice that must take place. For most, it will not be an easy journey. Reordering our lives and the life of the church around a missional-incarnational calling will seem too risky for some. They will prefer to remain on the sidelines, while others venture into the unfamiliar. But be assured on one thing. God is already there.

- Section Two -

FOSTERING A
MISSIONAL POSTURE

(What Steps Are Necessary?)

2

Stop and Go

Rhythms of Inner Formation

Lance Ford

• • •

And he said to them, "Go into all the world and
proclaim the gospel to the whole creation."

MARK 16:15 ESV

And I myself will send upon you what my Father has promised.
But you must wait in the city until the power
from above comes down upon you.

LUKE 24:49 GNT

The higher goal of spiritual living is not
to amass a wealth of information,
but to face sacred moments.

ABRAHAM HESCHEL

Several years ago, a few days before Christmas, my wife and I were finishing up our shopping. It was late in the evening and our son and a load of gifts filled the back seat and hatchback area of our car. We were waiting at a traffic light to cross four lanes in order to enter a shopping center on the other side of the highway. Like many guys, I am a somewhat aggressive driver and had my foot ready to go from brake to gas pedal in a split second as I kept my eyes on the traffic light, waiting for it to go from red to green. As soon as that light went to green I would blast out of the starting blocks.

Chuck Berry was crooning "Run, Run, Rudolph" on our car radio while I impatiently tapped the steering wheel, thinking of nothing but the light changing, when suddenly a strong impression streaked through my mind: "Do not go when the light changes to green." It was very clear. But it was also totally counterintuitive to my normal driving MO. Every stoplight has always been a competition to me, regardless of whether I was driving my classic '66 Mustang or a four-cylinder Honda.

My first reaction to the idea of "Don't go" was that it must have come from my own mind. But the more I wrestled and tried to dismiss the thought, the louder it became: "Do not go when the light changes to green!" I saw the light for the cars crossing in front of me change from green to yellow. This meant that in a second or so they would get a red light and mine would turn green. I readied myself to win another start. As soon as my light went green I hit the gas pedal—then just as quickly hit the brakes.

Our car lurched to a stop, and just as it did a car whizzed past in front of us at 50 miles an hour, running its red light. If I had proceeded across the intersection, my wife and son would have both taken a direct hit from the oncoming vehicle. I have no doubt that the Holy Spirit saved my family that evening.

Ours is a go-go-go culture. It is a society that places emphasis on immediacy and results. The idea is that very little good can come from stopping. To waste time is to waste money and probably to miss out on opportunity. We have been programmed to be doing something at all times. We are also programmed to not miss out on anything. There is so much information available that we are afraid we might fail to hear the latest something about somebody, or we might not catch the "breaking news" as quickly as possible after it takes place—or even while it takes place. A huge reason for the massive number of newspaper failures (many that have been printed daily for well over a century) in the last few years is that there is nothing "new" in printed news. In *Hyperculture: The Human Cost of Speed*, author Stephen Bertman uses "warp speed" as a metaphor for our contemporary lifestyle:

> First, warp speed disengages us from the past. The speed of our ascent leaves the past far behind us, like a receding landscape viewed from the rear of a roaring rocket, a landscape so progressively miniaturized by increasing velocity that its features lose all recognizable form. Traditions become incomprehensible; history, irrelevant; memories, a blur. Second, warp speed plunges us toward the future. The features of the future rush toward us like the fireballs of a meteor storm, blinding us to what lies farther ahead hidden in the cosmic night. Brilliant inventions, glittering products, glistening data, and luminous celebrities—each swarm brighter than the last—sweep past us in successive waves, dazzling our eyes. Nullifying a vision of the past and negating a true view of the future, warp speed isolates us in the present.[1]

The major emphasis of the missional movement is the sent nature of our calling as the body of Christ—going into culture with the gospel, practicing and proclaiming the good news of the kingdom of God. However, it is incumbent on us that we not lose our grip on the truth that we cannot go out under our own strength, understanding or power. To rely upon savvy, reason and human talent is to invite trouble along the way of mission.

We cannot go out under our own strength, understanding or power.

As the message of "go" takes root across the fields of the North American church, we have much reason to be encouraged. The listening ear of the body of Christ has been renewed as she hearkens to the call of God to fulfill the Great Commission. So it may seem ironic to some that in this chapter we are calling for a moment of stopping. After all, we're working hard to help our churches get going on mission. And it is the "go" (Mk 16:15) aspect of the Great Commission that the missional movement is primarily focused on. But we must not forget the "wait" (Lk 24:49) commandment of Jesus. The power of the Holy Spirit is essential lest we go in our own strength and intellect. Jesus called the Holy Spirit the Comforter. But he does not come for the sake of making us comfortable. The Holy Spirit comes to comfort us as we live out our mission as God's good news people.

KEEPING THE WELL CLEAN

What is the value of well-trained and well-informed Christians and spiritual leaders when their hearts remain ignorant? What is the value of great theological erudition or great pastoral adeptness or intense but fleeting mystical experience or social activism when there is not a well-formed heart to guide a well-formed life?
—Henri Nouwen, Michael Christensen and Rebecca Laird, *Spiritual Formation*

As helpful as it is, the term "spiritual formation" can sometimes mislead us into compartmentalizing inner heart formation as a lone category. This is erroneous because the entirety of our relationship with God is spiritual formation. Good deeds in the name of Jesus is spiritual formation. Sacrificial giving is spiritual formation. The entire process of discipleship is spiritual formation. Inner formation has to do with the shaping of our inner being—our heart for God and others and a listening ear to the voice of God. Maintaining a "right heart" means everything for anyone who hopes to go on mission. Solomon advises, "Above all else, guard your heart, for everything you do flows from it" (Prov 4:23). The following words from Dallas Willard provide a helpful commentary on this verse:

> Those with a well-kept heart are persons who are prepared for and capable of responding to the situations of life in ways that are good and right. Their will functions as it should, to choose what is good and avoid what is evil, and the other components of their nature cooperate to that end. They need not be "perfect"; but what all people manage in at least a few times and areas of life, they manage in life as a whole.[2]

Every spiritual revival that has shaken cities or nations started as a microrevival in the hearts of men and women. Spiritual awakening is a change of heart before it is a change of society and institutions. Anyone who lays stake to the moniker of "spiritual leader," which includes all pastors, must of all things be leading in the ways of shaping right hearts. When we fail to nourish our interior life we become susceptible to the onslaught of pride, ego, power abuse and a myriad of vices. Eventually our tanks run dry and we shift from working with the Lord to working for the Lord. We find ourselves operating almost entirely from our own fleshly base, regardless of our preaching, teaching, worship leading and other leadership activities. The joy of the Lord wanes, and our strength goes with it. We become proverbial "human doings" rather than "human beings."

It is incumbent on leadership teams to work together in the architecture of the rhythms of inner spiritual formation. As author James Wilhoit has written, we need an "intentional communal process of growing in our relationship with God and becoming conformed to Christ through the power of the Holy Spirit."[3] As leaders who are hoping to see our churches and communities transformed through missional engagement, we must ruthlessly evaluate the fruit of our belief in and reliance upon the Holy Spirit.

> **We must ruthlessly evaluate the fruit of our belief in and reliance upon the Holy Spirit.**

Franciscan priest Richard Rohr writes, "We're a people always rushing into the future because we're not experiencing a wholeness in the present."[4] For our churches to successfully navigate the missional quest, we as leaders must be honest about our belief in the power and necessity of the Spirit for our own individual lives and the lives of our co-laborers. This is a must before we can even begin to evaluate our churches as a whole. It is not the place for pastors or other leaders to dictate and prescribe spiritual formation rhythms and practices. But it is the responsibility of the leader to set the pace by example. The leader's task is to cultivate and nurture an atmosphere that is conducive to inner formation while being on the lookout for barriers that hinder opportunities for team members to develop their inner lives.

A few years ago my wife and I started a new garden on a large plot on our fifteen-acre hobby farm. After spending a bone-rattling week tilling the virgin soil, I was convinced we were ready to plant. In my mind all that stood between me and a bowl full of cornmeal-fried okra was the planting of the seeds. I was wrong. Big-time wrong. After five days of having every bone and tooth in my body shaken by the tiller, I told my wife she could start planting.

"Not so fast," she said. "The soil has to be analyzed. We'll probably have to do some amending first." I didn't know what amending meant, but I was pretty sure it had something to do with using the killer tiller again. When my wife returned from the county horticulturist with the results on the state of our soil, the report was less than pleasing. The bottom line was that I would be spending another couple of weeks blending several components into the soil in order for it to produce fruit.

It is not enough to have chosen good seed and a garden spot. Like a master gardener who analyzes the soil, removes rocks, stumps and weeds, and adds necessary ingredients to give the seed its best possible chance at producing fruit, leaders cultivate their ministry fields. Many church personnel policies and procedures are unnecessary stumps and rocks that hinder spiritual heart development. If space is not allowed for the land to rest and be nurtured when needed, the leadership is not proving itself wise.

STEPS ON THE QUEST

Begin working as a team to assess the current status of inner formation among your group. Start a regular time of discussion by asking these questions: What has been your greatest joy and your greatest frustration surrounding spiritual formation? What does your week look like in relation to spiritual formation? In what ways could we encourage one another in this area?

Spirit-Driven

When I was serving as the director of a church-planting center that was a ministry of a large church, I picked up my guitar one morning to spend a few minutes in worship. One of the guys in the office next to mine knocked and asked if he could join me. The following morning the same thing happened and the guy in the office on the other side of mine asked if he could join us as well. Over the next few weeks, first thing after arriving at our office complex, the three of us would grab our coffee and gather in my office where we spent about twenty minutes in worship and spontaneous prayer. It was incredibly empowering and set the tone for our day. Each of us spent time earlier in the morning in our homes in private devotions, or what some people refer to as quiet time. This time together was on top of that.

About four weeks into what had begun as a serendipitous time of worship, the three of us—all leaders of major ministry initiatives in the church—had settled into a wonderfully enriching rhythm of daily communion in the Spirit. One morning my office phone buzzed and the executive pastor asked if I could chat with him for a few minutes. I made my way into his office and he said he'd heard that the three of us guys had been spending a bit of morning time "singing." I shared with him how it began and how enriching it was. Quite frankly, I thought he was bringing this up because he was about to ask if he could join us. That was not the case. The executive pastor told me we would have to either stop doing this on "church time" or come in earlier and do it on our "own" time.

The issue for the executive pastor was that the time the three of us were spending being filled with the Spirit was not considered productive. It was not measurable. This underscores a serious malady. Many contemporary church leadership cultures, overly influenced by modernity, believe that what cannot be measured does not exist, or at the very most merits little value in comparison to tangible and immediate results. I remember hearing the late John Wimber (architect of the Vineyard Church movement) say, "Most pastors are constantly asking, 'How's business?' They have forgotten the first question—which is 'What business are we in?'" The reality is that we are in the Father's business, and the foremost thing we must do is abide in him if we have any hope to abound for him. Seminary professor Paul Jensen writes this:

> The collapse of space and time . . . can be viewed as a part of an addictive disease that has infected postmodern society and its institutions, including the church, much as a virus infects a computer hard drive. When the virus sufficiently infects church and mission structures, its addictive pace leaves insufficient time and space for God in its operations, especially its leadership structures. Organizations with schedules crowded in God's name leave people empty of fullness. God's activity and fullness get frozen out. Though the machine continues its active pace, the organism of the Spirit becomes paralyzed. Like a workaholic, the organization becomes powerless over its addictive pace and needs God to free it from sick patterns. It needs treatment.[5]

We do need treatment. We need the constant treatment of the Holy Spirit. As Jensen notes, too often our crowded schedules push away the Holy Spirit and drown out his voice. Our going must always be preceded by stopping—to be renewed and filled with the Spirit, not merely focused on strategic sharpness, intellectual aptitude and creative ideas, as helpful as those are.

I was unsure of how to go about this, and felt totally inadequate—I was scared to death, if you want the truth of it—and so nothing I said could have impressed you or anyone else. But the Message came through anyway. God's Spirit and God's power did it, which made it clear that your life of faith is a response to God's power, not to some fancy mental or emotional footwork by me or anyone else. (1 Cor 2:3-5 *The Message*)

In recent years many churches have adopted almost wholesale the manuals of the corporate business world as to staff protocol and policy. Time off—vacation time, sick days or personal days—is determined by the "employee" manual, which is usually crafted from bits and pieces of business-world human resource departments. In effect we have supplanted the wisdom of the Word with the wisdom of the world. We have bought into a misguided and devastating notion that attempts to squeeze biblical spirituality out of Westernized wineskins.

Too often we buy into the deception that it's wasteful not to fill our schedules with activity. This is not only shortsighted; it is blindness to the fuel source of genuine spirituality. We have been both proud and deceived as we carry on our busy lives. Henri Nouwen said,

It requires an enormous human effort to be and to stay in the world with its many demands while keeping our hearts and minds solidly anchored in God. The various disciplines of the spiritual life are meant for freedom and are reliable means for the creation of helpful boundaries in our lives within which God's voice can be heard, God's presence felt, and God's guidance experienced. Without such boundaries that make space for God, our lives quickly narrow down; we hear and see less and less, we become spiritually sick, and we become one-dimensional, and sometimes delusional, people.[6]

Planning margin into our lives in terms of open blocks of time is essential to all spiritual development. Church staffs need it on multiple levels across personal and corporate schedules: daily, weekly, monthly and yearly. When we intentionally schedule time for nothingness—just being with Jesus, sitting at his feet like Mary Magdalene (who so frustrated Martha by her lack of busyness)—we are setting a place at the table of our hearts for the Lord to commune with us. We are saying to Jesus, "Your heart, your hands, your eyes, your ears are all bigger, better and more efficient and trustworthy than mine." This is about trust, the true essence of walking in faith. Nouwen writes,

> The world says, "If you are not making good use of your time, you are useless." Jesus says: "Come spend some useless time with me." If we can detach ourselves from the idea of the usefulness of prayer and the results of prayer, we become free to "waste" a precious hour with God in prayer. Gradually, we may find, our "useless" time will transform us, and everything around us will be different. Prayer is being unbusy with God instead of being busy with other things. To not be useful is to remind myself that if anything important or fruitful happens through prayer, it is God who achieves the result.[7]

We don't trek the pages of the Gospels for long without seeing Jesus leading his disciples into retreats of space and time for the sake of inner formation. He would often invite them to join him on getaways. At times it was in one of their homes or on a mountaintop, an upper room, a garden, a boat, a shoreline or a walk through a wheat field. A lifestyle void of habits that take us into retreats of space and time leaves us open to the whims of the kinds of space and time that deform our lives to begin with.

Rhythms of Grace

Just as with breathing—slowly in, slowly out—it is essential that we orchestrate our lives in a rhythm of "stop and go" so that mission flows out of a constant connection to the heart and voice of God. Eugene Peterson calls this the "unforced rhythms of grace" and it is a wonderful tune for this dance called life.

> Come to me. Get away with me and you'll recover your life. I'll show you how to take a real rest. Walk with me and work with me—watch how I do it. Learn the unforced rhythms of grace. (Mt 11:28 *The Message*)

Jesus wasn't just preaching here. He was speaking from what he lived. Jesus was well aware that his incarnational plunge into the brokenness of humanity necessitated soul care for himself and his disciples. It was necessary for him to embrace the spiritual formation processes and patterns that any man or woman who hopes to connect with God must do. Jesus followed a self-imposed habit of discipline that frequently took him away from the crowds and ministry into solitude, rest and prayer, both alone and in the small company of his twelve disciples. Keith Meyer underscores Jesus' commitment to this pattern of soul maintenance:

> He needed soul care just as we do. In the humility of his incarnation he had to submit to the same processes of spiritual growth and maturation as we do, and his soul-care rhythms involved the discipline of disengaging from life and ministry to be with the Father, where he was formed by the Spirit in the Father's love. Jesus' interactive life with the Father, evidenced by the short conversational prayers and his frequent references to his Father's authority, power and voice as he ministered, was the fruit of disengaging from life as usual in order to be alone and enriched by the Spirit and the Father.[8]

Table 2.1, citing passages from Mark's Gospel, is a brief eye-opening sampling of the correlation between Jesus' frequent withdrawals from the masses and his empowered mission in both deed and word. His communion with the Holy Spirit, whether alone or with others, fueled his ministry engagement.

Table 2.1. Jesus' Pattern of Soul Maintenance

Withdrawal	Empowerment
Mark 1:11-13 Retreats to wilderness, is tempted. *Alone*	**Mark 1:14-34** Begins public ministry. Proclaims the gospel. Calls his disciples. Heals people and casts out demons.
Mark 1:35 Prays early in the morning. *Alone*	**Mark 1:36–3:16** Preaches in synagogues. Casts out demons. Heals people.
Mark 3:13-19 Goes up the mountain with the Twelve. *Community*	**Mark 3:2–5:43** Teaches. Calms the storm. Casts out demons. Performs multiple healings.
Mark 6:30-37 Goes to solitary place for rest with the Twelve (interrupted). *Community*	**Mark 6:38-44** Walks on water, calms storm. Feeds the five thousand-plus.
Mark 6:45-52 Prays in the night on the mountainside. *Alone*	**Mark 6:53-56** Many are healed by touching him.
Mark 9:2 Retreats to mountaintop with three disciples. *Community*	**Mark 9:2** Experiences transfiguration. Encounters Elijah and Moses.

The key to the expansive growth of the church as well as the extraordinary miracles, deep fellowship and generosity we read about in the book of Acts was the rhythm of life practiced by the followers of Jesus. They operated in a red-light/green-light rhythm of listening to the voice of the Lord through prayer and the Word of God and moving out under the influence of the Holy Spirit. Across the landscape of the book of Acts we see the early disciples living a "stop and go" lifestyle. These early Jesus-

Table 2.2. "Stop and Go" in Acts

Withdrawal	Empowerment
Acts 1:12-25 120 gather in the Upper Room. *Community*	**Acts 1:26** Matthias appointed as one of the Twelve.
Acts 2:1 Believers wait on the Lord in solitude. *Community*	**Acts 2:14-41** Peter proclaims, preaches. Three thousand souls added.
Acts 2:42 Believers in habit of prayer, fellowship, meal sharing, teaching. *Community*	**Acts 2:43-47** Apostles perform signs, wonders. Believers share possessions. Salvations occur daily.
Acts 3:1 Peter and John participate in temple prayer hour. *Community*	**Acts 3:2–4:4** Peter and John perform healing miracle. Peter preaches, proclaims the gospel. Five thousand new believers added.
Acts 4:23-30 Believers gather in prayer. *Community*	**Acts 4:31-35** Believers filled with Spirit. Word of God proclaimed with boldness. Believers experience unity. Possessions shared. Atmosphere of grace develops. No needy among the believers.
Acts 6:1-6 The Twelve and company of believers gather in prayer. *Community*	**Acts 6:7** Proclamation of the Word increases. Disciples multiply significantly. Priests converted.
Acts 9:8-12 Saul (Paul) waits and prays, fasting. *Alone*	**Acts 9:10-18** Ananias obeys God and goes to Saul. Saul's eyes healed. Saul filled with Holy Spirit and baptized.
Acts 13:1-3 Antioch church leaders worship, fast, pray. *Community*	**Acts 13:2-5** Holy Spirit gives instructions. Barnabas and Saul sent in power of Holy Spirit. Gospel proclaimed in synagogues.
Acts 14:23 Paul, Barnabas, company of believers gather in prayer, fast. *Community*	**Acts 14:23-27** Elders appointed. Gospel proclaimed through broad region.
Acts 16:25 Paul, Silas pray and sing hymns. *Community*	**Acts 16:26-34** Prison shaken. Jailer converted, household saved.
Acts 16:25 Paul, Silas pray and sing hymns. *Community*	**Acts 18:9-11** Paul receives boldness. Paul teaches the Word for a year and half, strengthening Corinthian church.

followers did so both individually and corporately.

It is clear that the first missional people, the apostles and early Christians, danced the rhythms of inner formation. Frequency of prayer, fasting, shared meals and worship fueled their world-changing mission. Both Jesus and the apostles observed fixed hours of prayer, Sabbath keeping, getaways of solitude and the joy of the Jewish feasts and festivals. Unlike most of us today, these folks frequently broke away from the prison of productivity and did a lot of time wasting!

CRAZY BUSY

> *The first missional people, the apostles and early Christians, danced the rhythms of inner formation.*

Though it is highly aggrandized, there is nothing noble about the current state of the American work ethic. Furthermore, church personnel policies drawn and designed after the American work ethic are senseless and lacking in biblical wisdom, thumbing their noses at a biblical work-rest ethic pattern. For example, in 2010 the average employed American worker was entitled to eighteen vacation days but used only fourteen of them. Alternatively, workers in France received thirty-seven vacation days and used thirty-five of them, while the average worker in Great Britain received twenty-eight vacation days and took twenty-five.[9] The average vacation time in Australia is twenty-eight calendar days. According to one recent survey, fifty-seven percent of working Americans will have unused vacation time at the end of the year, and while most workers say they deserve to take that time off, many also admit having reservations about asking their bosses for a vacation.[10]

A myriad of reasons and excuses are (and will continue to be) served up by church leaders for following lock-step with the ways of the host culture. Our point here is for church leaders to take the lead in recalibrating to Jesusian ways of living. Not only will a movement to a biblical work-rest ethic serve church staffs well but it will also provide witness and a pattern for Christian business owners to follow. For evidence, look to the success of Chick-fil-A restaurants. Founder Truett Cathy's policy of closing his stores on Sundays for the purpose of "giving employees Sunday off as a day for family, worship, fellowship or rest"[11] is not a bad argument for the merit of trusting God to make up the difference when valuable time is "wasted." The company website provides the following explanation for the frequently asked question as to why the restaurants are closed on Sunday:

> In today's business world, the Closed-on-Sunday policy may seem to be a costly business decision. But, as company sales figures have consistently proven, Chick-fil-A restaurants often generate more business per square foot in six days than many other quick-service restaurants produce in seven. Chick-fil-A generated more than $4 billion in sales in 2011, and the chain has enjoyed sales gains for 44 consecutive years (every year since the first Chick-fil-A restaurant opened in 1967). Cathy credits "blessings from the Lord" for the great success the company has enjoyed, and he remains as committed as ever to maintaining the Closed-on-Sunday policy. "I feel it's the best business decision I ever made," says Cathy.[12]

Missional community leader Sean Gladding says, "To take a day of rest is to resist the internal forces that drive us to assert ourselves through our activity. It is to refuse to conform to the restlessness of the culture we find ourselves in, to cease our tireless striving to reshape the world in our own image."[13] Of the many reasons we have been given the Sabbath, refreshing our bodies is just one. Rabbi Abraham Heschel writes:

> To the biblical mind . . . labor is the means toward an end, and the Sabbath as a day of rest, as a day of abstaining from

toil, is not for the purpose of recovering one's lost strength and becoming fit for the forthcoming labor. The Sabbath is a day for the sake of life. Man is not a beast of burden, and the Sabbath is not for the purpose of enhancing the efficiency of his work. "Last in creation, first in intention," the Sabbath is "the end of creation of heaven and earth." The Sabbath is not for the sake of the weekdays; the weekdays are for the sake of Sabbath. It is not an interlude but the climax of living.[14]

Author Dan Allender notes that thirty-seven percent of Americans take fewer than seven days off per year and only fourteen percent take vacations of two weeks or longer. Americans take the shortest paid vacations in the world, and twenty percent of those who do take time off stay in touch with the office.[15] As un-American as it sounds, Sabbath observance means we schedule one day of doing nothing into our week. The first tenet of the Westminster Catechism is, "The chief end of man is to glorify God and to enjoy him forever." Forever begins here and now.

WASTING TIME

Sabbath observance means we schedule one day of doing nothing into our week.

Growing up as a Jew, Jesus would have participated in Israel's spiritual practices, which included daily, weekly, monthly and yearly observances. When we add up all of the "chill" time the typical Jesus-era Jew spent, it is significant. Certain parts of these times were to be, in the words of Zechariah, "joyful and glad occasions and happy festivals" (Zech 8:19). In contemporary vernacular—they partied. Other occasions were marked by deeper solemnity and silence. We see a mixture of rhythms in how these times were observed in demeanor, as well as in solitude or community. Regardless of the way the time was spent, the fre-

quency of "wasted" time by Jesus and his contemporaries is remarkable when we consider it.

Daily. The Shema was Israel's central confession, given by
Moses to the Israelites near the end of their forty years of wilderness wanderings.[16] Since the time it was pronounced by
Moses, three times per day Jews have recited, "Hear O Israel:
The LORD our God, the LORD is one. You shall love the LORD your
God with all your heart and with all your soul and with all your
might" (Deut 6:4-5 ESV). Shema means "to hear," which evokes
the concept of silence or intense listening for God's voice in
prayer. Along with praying the Shema, devout Jews had a habit
of a fixed hour prayer in the morning, afternoon and evening.[17]

Weekly. Jesus grew up attending Sabbath services in the
temple, and though he redefined Sabbath based on his lordship,
he still participated in Sabbath keeping. We turn again to the
words of Abraham Heschel:

> He who wants to enter the holiness of the day must first
> lay down the profanity of clattering commerce, of being
> yoked to toil. He must go away from the screech of dis-
> sonant days, from the nervousness and fury of acquisi-
> tiveness and the betrayal in embezzling his own life. He
> must say farewell to manual work and learn to understand
> that the world has already been created and will survive
> without the help of man. Six days a week we wrestle with
> the world, wringing profit from the earth; on the Sabbath
> we especially care for the seed of eternity planted in the
> soul. The world has our hands, but our soul belongs to
> Someone Else. Six days a week we seek to dominate the
> world, on the seventh day we try to dominate the self.[18]

Hearkening to the call of the Sabbath is to respond to the invitation into nonproductivity. What could be more anti-

American? Pete Scazzero says, "The Sabbath calls us to build the doing of nothing into our schedules each week. Nothing measurable is accomplished. By the world's standards it is inefficient, unproductive, and useless."[19] Just as the Israelites could not gather manna on the Sabbath, we are called to cease providing for ourselves and instead trust the Lord. The essence of Sabbath is that God says, "Today is on me. Rest and enjoy your life, your family and your friends. I'm picking up the tab."

Monthly. With calendars based on lunar cycles as well as solar, a regular part of Jewish life during the time of Jesus included observance of monthly new moon festivals. Celebrations took place on the fourth, fifth, seventh and tenth months. The light of the new moon broke through a time of darkness, pointing to the hope that God would bring deliverance and light after the darkness of exile and judgment.

Yearly. In addition to Hanukkah and the feast of Purim, devout Jews observed three major feasts during the lifetime of Jesus. Passover was the spring festival that celebrated the escape from Egypt. Pentecost took place in early summer, celebrating the giving of the Torah, and the Feast of Tabernacles was a celebration of God's provision during the wilderness sojourn.

So how can all this Jewish background inform us as twenty-first-century Western Christians? How might we draw on these ancient habits to craft our own rhythms of inner formation toward Christlikeness? In addition to weekly Sabbath observance, we should weave daily, monthly and annual times for renewal, rest, refreshment and relaxation into our normal life pattern. We suggest the following:

> *We should weave daily, monthly and annual times for renewal, rest, refreshment and relaxation into our normal life pattern.*

Daily office. The daily office is a reference to what some people call "fixed-hour prayer." Saint

Benedict said, "To pray is to work, to work is to pray." This statement "gave form to another of the great, informing concepts of Christian spirituality—the inseparability of spiritual life from physical life."[20] When most of us hear the word *office* we think of a place rather than an activity. We go to the office building. We work at an office. But we also use the word in phrases such as "running for office" or "holding office." So the activity-related definition of the word is not far from our minds. The daily office provides us with a structure for reconnecting with the Lord throughout our day. Typically four times are set aside for this purpose: morning, midday, evening and bedtime (compline). Some people use the Book of Common Prayer, others use more contemporary resources such as Phyllis Tickle's *Divine Hours*. Other folks create their own form of daily office, usually made from a menu of psalms, hymns, the Lord's Prayer and readings of Scripture passages. Here Henri Nouwen shares his:

> For morning prayers, I have a simple formula that anyone can follow. I read three Psalms out loud, and then a reading from the New Testament, followed by ten minutes of silent meditation. Then I pray another Psalm and read a contemporary text of some sort, followed by another ten minutes of silence. Then I pray a concluding prayer and the Our Father. It takes less than one hour, and the nice thing about such a format is that I can always invite a friend: "This is what I do in the mornings, would you like to join me?"[21]

Monthly retreats. Earlier we considered how the Gospels reveal many instances of Jesus getting away—sometimes by himself, at other times with a group of three or his entire posse of twelve disciples. Retreats (both alone and in groups) for a day or two each month for the purpose of meditation or recreation are both wise and healthy for the soul. You may have a place in mind or you may have a friend or family member who has a weekend cabin or lake house you would be welcome to use. The bottom line is to find a place, schedule the time away and go for it.

Vacations. A great starting place for pastors and church staffs is to follow the ancient Jewish pattern of no less than three times per year of extended time for festival (i.e., a vacation). Break away from the crazy policies that provide only a week or two of vacation time. Think outside of the conventional American HR boxes. Set your team up to win and as a pattern for others to follow.

Sabbaticals. Many colleges and seminaries provide sabbaticals of one kind or another to their faculty. And there are examples of corporations that offer sabbaticals at certain levels as well. The church should be leading the field in this area. A good friend of ours was on sabbatical as we wrote this. The policy at his church is for ministry staff members to receive a three-month sabbatical after the initial seven years of service. Sabbaticals take place every five years after that. No work responsibility is to take place during this time, and ministry-related emails are suspended during the sabbaticals. It is to be a true period of rest and recreation.

STEPS ON THE QUEST

Set aside the necessary undistracted time for your leadership team to analyze personal and corporate schedules. What rhythms are in place for staff and volunteers? Do you see regular periods of scheduled margin? Are there blocked out times for being with the Lord just as there are blocked out times for doing for the Lord? Look at the personnel policies of your church or ministry in relation to days off and vacation days. Have they been scripted biblically or conscripted from the ways of the world? Ask the hard question: Does your church personnel policy encourage or inhibit opportunities for inner formation?

We are aware that this lone chapter on the subject doesn't allow us to give near the amount of discussion needed regarding the ways, means and modes of inner formation. Thankfully the Lord has provided a great number of men and women who have practiced and written tremendously helpful treatises on the subject. For readers who want to dig further we suggest you would do well to read the works of the authors we have cited in this chapter.

3

AD *30 All Over Again*

Emphasizing Missionary Formation

Brad Brisco

• • •

The whole congregation and every individual within it
belong with all their powers and potentialities
to the mission of God's kingdom

JÜRGEN MOLTMANN

A small body of determined spirits fired by
an unquenchable faith in their mission
can alter the course of history.

MAHATMA GANDHI

I received a phone call not long ago from a pastor at a
church that was experiencing some difficult times. He had

been at the church for ten years, and over that time the church had seen a steady decline in attendance. The pastor knew I worked with new church plants in the region and was hoping to learn what these churches were doing to reach new people.

Specifically, he asked what times most of the new churches were meeting on Sunday mornings. His congregation wanted to reach young families and what he referred to as "twenty-some-things," and they had concluded that if they moved their Sunday morning worship time from 10:30 a.m. to 11 a.m., they would be in a better position to do so. They believed that younger adults wanted to sleep in on Sundays and that the delayed starting time would open the door for them to attend their church. This congregation was operating under the dangerous assumption that the greatest barrier keeping people from their church was the time slot of their Sunday service. They failed to recognize that the vast majority of people in their community had absolutely no interest in what was taking place in their church building on Sunday morning, regardless of the time.

This conversation illustrates the reality that Christendom continues to maintain a stranglehold on much of the American church. When we use the term *Christendom* we are referring to the alliance between church and state that was established in fourth-century Europe. It dominated European thinking for more than a thousand years and still impacts the way Christians think and act today, despite the obvious erosion of that church-state alliance.

As leaders we must first help the church realize that we no longer live in a Christian society. The church in America does not hold the place of influence it once did. Second, as we come to grips with the fact that the mission field—which was once thought to exist only in faraway places—has now come to our own backyard, we will begin to rightly see ourselves as missionaries. In this chapter we will first briefly survey the Christendom-to-post-Christendom shift and its implications on the church today. Then we will discuss how to equip and deploy every member as a missionary into our newly established mission field.

FROM THE MIDDLE TO THE MARGINS

There are numerous factors that have influenced the change we see today in American society and as a result have complicated the interplay between church and culture. Issues such as globalization, urbanization, economic crises and the rise of the information age have all had a significant impact on the church. However, nothing has shaken the foundations of the church over the centuries as much as the rise and fall of Christendom.

In AD 313, the Roman emperor Constantine adopted the Christian faith as his own and decided to replace paganism with Christianity as the official imperial religion. As Stuart Murray notes, "He invited the church to come in from the margins of society, where it had been operating for the previous three centuries, and join him in Christianizing the empire."[1] Supplying great resources and favors to the church, Constantine set in motion a process that would eventually bring all of Europe into a church-state relationship known as Christendom.[2] It is difficult to overstate the impact Constantine's decision had on the Christian faith. Christendom meant:

- The assumption that all citizens were Christian by birth
- The development of a "sacral society" where there was no effective distinction between religion and politics
- Infant baptism as the symbol of necessary incorporation into the Christian society
- The imposition of a supposedly "Christian morality" on the entire population (although normally Old Testament moral standards were applied)

- Sunday as the required day of church attendance, with penalties for noncompliance

- The definition of orthodoxy as the common belief shared by all, which was determined by powerful church leaders supported by the state

- The construction of massive and ornate church buildings

- A strong distinction between clergy and laity, and the relegation of the laity to a largely passive role

- The increased wealth of the church and the obligation of required tithes to fund the system

- The division of the globe into Christendom and heathendom and the waging of war in the name of Christ and the church

- The use of political and military force to impose the Christian faith.[3]

The foundation of the Christendom system was a close partnership between the church and government. The church provided religious legitimacy to state activity, while the state delivered secular force to back up ecclesiastical decisions, no matter how unbiblical or unpopular those decisions were.

The net effect of Christendom over the centuries was that Christianity moved from being a vibrant, revolutionary, social and spiritual movement to becoming a static religious institution with its corresponding structures, priesthood and rituals. The Christian faith moved from being an integrated way of life that was lived out seven days a week to becoming an obligation that was fulfilled by attending a church meeting at a set time.

By the middle of the twentieth century, however, it was becoming clear in Europe that Christendom was in serious decline. People began to use the term *post-Christendom* to describe the church's loss of social privilege. Others used it to refer to Western civilizations that no longer considered themselves to be Christian.

In this era of post-Christendom the church once again returned to the margins of society, losing its position of prominence and control and returning to minority status. In post-Christendom the church has come full circle. It has shifted from living on the margins of society to an elevated place of power and control to once again being relegated to the margins. This shift can be illustrated in figure 3.1.

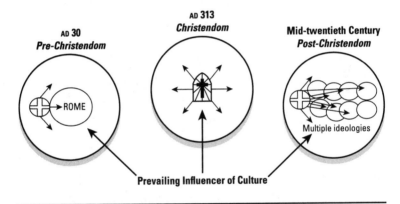

Figure 3.1. Shifts in the church's cultural prominence

Before Constantine, the prevailing influence on society was the Roman Empire and the church was a marginalized sect located on the outskirts. However, the early church was making serious inroads into the empire. During the time of Christendom, the church became the central influence on culture, though it was corrupted with political and military power. Today the church is once again relegated to the margins. And instead of a single, unifying cultural influence, there are multiple, sometimes intertwined ideologies that shape the way people think and behave. The influence of postmodernity, religious pluralism, consumerism, deinstitutionalization and information technology have all played a part in filling the void left by the crumbling of Christendom. Author Reggie McNeal refers to this time of transition as "AD 30 all over again."[4]

It is this displacement of the church to the margins that has caused such great angst for those in the church today. Many church people still believe that the church maintains a place of prominence in society. They assume that people still look to the church for guidance or answers. But it's like the car ads in the Sunday morning paper. If people aren't in the market for a car, they never even think about opening that portion of the paper. In fact, over time they don't even notice the ads exist.

The point is that the vast majority of de-churched and unchurched people are not looking for the things of the church. Most don't even know your church building is located where it is. It makes absolutely no difference if you change the times of your meetings, purchase a new sign or change the name of the church—they simply are not in the market for a church. And until the church comes to grips with this difficult reality, it will be impossible to make the necessary changes in the way the church thinks and acts. As one author has put it, "The legacy of Christendom has hobbled the church in responding to the vigorous challenge of modern culture to faith."[5]

> **The vast majority of de-churched and unchurched people are not looking for the things of the church.**

Lets be clear. Making cosmetic changes to the church facility or adding new signage to communicate more clearly is not bad or evil. But don't kid yourself. Such changes will not light a fire under the seat of those not interested in the church. They won't wake up on a Sunday morning and suddenly say, "Hey, I think we should go to that church down the street that just got a new sign." As surprising as it might be, the fact is they have probably never even noticed the sign!

STEPS ON THE QUEST

Do the people in your church understand how the religious landscape in North America has changed? Do they still think that lost people are open to attending the programs and activities of the church? Does Christendom maintain a stranglehold on the way they view the relationship between church and culture? Do they long for past "glory days" of the life of the church?

List the changes your church may need to make in order to connect with those who are no longer interested in things of the church. What steps will you take to help the church incorporate the first change?

Missionary Formation

What then is the appropriate response to the challenge? The solution is to recognize the church's relationship to the culture in terms of a missionary encounter. In other words, to see that in a post-Christendom context the church once again exists within an alien world. The mission field is no longer located somewhere else; instead it surrounds us on every side. And the greatest problem with making superficial changes is that we falsely assume those changes will somehow help the church grow. We therefore put our time and energy into those practices instead of equipping and releasing people into this new, rapidly growing mission field. There is no final answer or perfect solution to transitioning the existing church in a missional direction. But if there was one—a silver bullet—it would be the formation of every church member into a missionary.

God's people need to be empowered as agents of the king. We need to learn how to think as missionaries. Furthermore, we need to develop skills that will help us meaningfully engage people and places. These skills involve learning how to better identify and participate in God's activity wherever we live, work and play.

However, beyond equipping people with specific missional practices, the church must be prepared to freely release people into their missional calling. The church needs to give permission. In other words, it needs to say to its members that it is good to start new initiatives. It is right to take risks for the kingdom. It is okay to miss a church meeting when you are engaged in activities with those uninterested in the church. Kim Hammond, national director of the missional training organization Forge America, says missionary formation involves the giving of language and license. We must give people new missionary language, but we must also then give them the license to go and do what God has called them to. Which in most cases will not be located in the church but instead will be positioned in the world where God has already placed them in their everyday lives.

This unfortunately runs contrary to the kind of recruitment the church is used to. Reggie McNeal argues that the typical church strategy for recruiting and deploying people in the church is actually missionally counterproductive.

> Frequently pastors lament to me that they can't get their high-powered laypeople "involved." They almost always think about offering them church jobs to entice them. The idea that God has gifted people only for church jobs flies in the face of his redemptive mission in the world. We ask people to leave their place of greatest connection and in-

fluence (their homes, their businesses, their schools, their communities) to come to the church to do some church work! . . . I am not saying that ushering or serving on the finance committee are unimportant. It's just that limiting church member contributions to these responsibilities reflects a lack of missional awareness.

Laypeople see the disconnect in the "every member has a ministry" strategy. They are voting by not lending their time, energy, and money to ministry "vision" that has the church as the primary beneficiary or recipient. . . . Church ministry to them is an add-on activity to an already crowded life. They wonder why God can't use them where he has already embedded them—in their homes, workplaces, schools, and communities.[6]

Missionary formation means everyone gets to participate. Everyone *must* participate! The doctrine of the priesthood of the believer (which we will discuss further in chapter 7) is not merely about God's accessibility to all, it is also about advocating for God's calling on the lives of everyone. There are no professional missionaries. If the church were a sports team, we would say that no one is relegated to the bench. Everyone gets to play.

But instead the church has created an unbiblical clergy-laity divide that has kept the majority of the body of Christ on the sidelines. Missiologist Ed Stetzer states it this way:

> *Missionary formation means everyone gets to participate.*

My fear is that we have created a class system in the body of Christ comprised of the "called" and the "not so much called." Nothing could be further from the truth. The ministry assignment of the laypeople is not to simply "lay" around and tell the called what they should be doing. Laypeople are not to be customers of religious goods and services served by the storekeeper clergy. We are all called although our current assignments may vary dramatically.

Jesus said to an ordinary group of people, "As the Father has sent Me, I also send you" (John 20:21). These were not professionals, with the exception of professional fishermen and a professional tax collector. And if we hope to engage and evangelize the world with the gospel, we cannot possibly rely on professionals to do it.[7]

One of the problems, however, is that many people don't know they are really a part of the team. They haven't been told that they can play. There are hundreds if not thousands of people sitting in churches every week who are dying to be released into God's mission. They have never been in a church that encouraged them to be involved in activities outside of the church walls.

One morning Lance and I were meeting with the staff from New City Church, mentioned in chapter one, documenting some of the incredible stories of mission that were taking place through the people of the church. At one point just in passing, the children's director, Tiffany Mills, made a simple statement about missional engagement.

She was reflecting on her family's desire in the past, before becoming a part of New City, to engage in mission but never really having the support or the permission of their church to do so. She said she always knew there was more to the Christian life than attending church on Sunday and giving financially to church programs. But she never quite understood what it was she was called to do. At that point Tiffany said that she "was having a crisis of mission that felt like a crisis of faith."

We would contend that the church in America is bursting with people who feel the same way Tiffany did. The missionary impulse is latent within us all. It is part of being human and fully alive. In many cases people don't need to be motivated and inspired; they simply need to be given permission to go for it. And they need someone

> *The missionary impulse is latent within us all. It is part of being human, and fully alive.*

to go for it with them. We need to send the church to be the church where there is no church. And that must involve every single believer that makes up the church.

CAPTURING THE MISSIONAL IMAGINATION

Once people are equipped and released into the local context to which God has sent them, an important follow-up action will play an enormous role in moving the church in a missional direction. That is tapping into the power of individual stories.

As everyday Christians engage in God's mission, their personal stories need to be told. The church needs to hear stories of how others are impacting lives throughout the community. Stories of ordinary folks engaged in mission have incredible power. Stories act as a vehicle that drives our missional imaginations.

In the book *Made to Stick* the authors describe the power of stories as twofold. Stories provide simulation (the knowledge about how to act) and inspiration (the motivation to act).[8] Both are crucial for generating action. In other words, stories help people to "see." Stories have the ability to place listeners in a precise situation where they can gain a new vantage point. Through story they can now see what was once hidden from view.

But furthermore, stories can provide the motivation to act. Not only do stories make things more real than ever, but they allow the listener to say, "I can do that." Stories create new possibilities and energize people to do things they had not previously imagined.

Stories create new possibilities and energize people to do things they had not previously imagined.

Many times in the church we assume that people can be informed and motivated through facts. But stories have an innate ability that facts do not. Facts are not influential until they mean something to someone. We can share facts about the number of children in the foster system or the number of homeless people living on the streets of our city, but until people can see the problem and envision the solution—via story—there will be little action. If you want others to see what you have seen, then open their eyes by telling them stories.

I recently met with the leadership team from a large church that desired to better understand what it would take to move the church in a missional direction. When talking about the importance of capturing and telling the stories of people on mission, one of the staff members admitted that she didn't have any stories and believed the rest of the staff was probably in the same boat. She confessed that her time was spent exclusively with church people. The church's busy schedule left little room to spend time building relationships with those outside the church.

In almost the same breath she asked, "So where do I, or where do we as the staff, begin in transitioning this church?" The answer to her question was obvious. I said it must start by cultivating your own stories. You must live life in such a way that you have an abundance of stories of how God is leading you on a daily basis to participate in what he's doing in the lives of others. This doesn't mean that all of the stories have to be your personal experiences. But you as leaders on the missional quest had better be the ones who model what it means to be engaged in God's mission outside the confines of the church building. If you do not have your own stories to tell to your congregation, then it should be obvious: that is where you need to start the journey.

STEPS ON THE QUEST

Ask how you can capture the missional imagination of the people in your congregation. Where can the stories of the congregation be told? How can you incorporate stories into the corporate gatherings? Small groups? Social media?

4

Won't You Be My Neighbor?

Knowing and Loving the Ones We Live Among

Lance Ford

• • •

*One way of looking at a local block or a small neighborhood
is to see it as a bunch of people with problems and gifts.
The job of building community is to take the problems
out of the closet and open up the gifts.*

Peter Block

There are no strangers here; only friends you haven't yet met.

William Butler Yeats

*When Jesus was asked to reduce everything in the Bible into
one command he said: Love God with everything you have
and love your neighbor as yourself. What if he meant
that we should love our actual neighbors?
You know, the people who live right next door.*

Jay Pathak and Dave Runyon

Growing up in the sixties and seventies in a smallish North
Texas town, I consider myself fortunate to have been raised in
the best of two worlds. My hometown of Keller could be called
a small town-plus. At the time it was just a little burg, content
to be in the shadows of the Dallas-Fort Worth Metroplex.
Though it was a town of just a few thousand, the amenities of a
large city were accessible. Shopping malls, professional sports
teams and several colleges were close by. Life was good.

In the autumn of 1972 my family was the second to move
into a new subdivision, Indian Meadows, with affordable homes
for folks who were in a lower middle-class income bracket.
Central air conditioning, automatic dishwashers and fully
bricked houses were the selling points. Within a couple of years
about 125 homes stood where nothing but mesquite trees,
cotton-tail rabbits and anthills had once prevailed. A neighborhood was born.

Ours was a blue collar, working class neighborhood. Most of
the men carried a lunch pail to work, laboring as plumbers, car-
penters, mechanics or machinists at places like General Dy-
namics, Bell Helicopter (where my dad worked) or the General
Motors assembly plant. There were no doctors, lawyers or white
collar professionals in Indian Meadows. Affordable housing
meant single mothers were able to realize the dream of home-
ownership, along with young families who were just getting
started with their versions of the American Dream. It was like
we were all in it together—new starts and new leases on life—
and although sitting porches were not to be found in my neighborhood, people actually became neighborly. It didn't seem like
they had to try very hard to do it. It came natural.

Fast-forward to the second decade of the new millennium
and we find ourselves having to work extremely hard to have a

neighborhood of neighbors. Our lives move at techno speed and our minds are warped by disengagement. Philip Langdon, author of *A Better Place to Live*, laments this conundrum as he reflects on his frequent bike rides through a neighborhood near his own suburban home:

> I bike through a residential area that includes a large undeveloped property continually strewn with trash and broken trees. The people who live in the vicinity seem unable to get the owner or the town to clean it up—and seem incapable of organizing to clean it up themselves. When I bike past the area, it occurs to me that this is not a neighborhood; it is only a collection of unconnected individuals.[1]

Langdon's last sentence is haunting. Sit down with just about any group of Americans and they will tell you they long to live in a neighborly neighborhood but they don't know how to do it. Connecting naturally seems so—well, unnatural. The lack of a community experience perpetuates the middle-class psyche of individualism and privacy. And it grows in the petri dish of safety and security. In our heads we have come to believe that independence is and should be normal. In our hearts we know better. We long for connection with others. In our deepest parts we are aware that normal life should be carried out interdependently.

For Christ-followers it is especially important that we lean into the community that is the living, breathing, tangible body of Christ and recognize the light it shines to a world wrapped in the throes of darkness. The typical Christian may not be a church planter in the traditional sense of the word, but she certainly can be a neighborhood cultivator. Every home on

In our heads we have come to believe that independence is and should be normal. In our hearts we know better.

our street, every apartment in our building contains individuals and families that matter. They matter every bit as much as you and I matter. The myriad concerns, fears, anxieties, hopes, dreams and longings that traffic in our own hearts are doing the same in every household around us. Who will be the ones to engage the disengaged—to connect the unconnected?

Loving Starts with Knowing

Take a look at the following chart. A doctor would preface this by saying, "This might hurt a little." Jay Pathak and Dave Runyon use this exercise to help people gain a realistic picture of where they are as to knowing their neighborhood. Start by picturing the grid as a plat of your own neighborhood. The middle box is your house or apartment and the other eight boxes represent the residences closest to where you live. Concentrate on those eight boxes that represent the homes of others around you. Fill in the information for each letter in each box:

Pathak and Runyon say that only about ten percent of people can come up with the names of all eight of their neighbors, about three percent can provide information for line "b" for every home, and only one percent can fill out line "c" for each residence.

STEPS ON THE QUEST

Issue the challenge to your small groups and leadership team to work through the neighborhood grid. Have them gather in groups and do the exercise. Ask the groups to discuss ways to respond to the results of the neighborhood grid exercise.

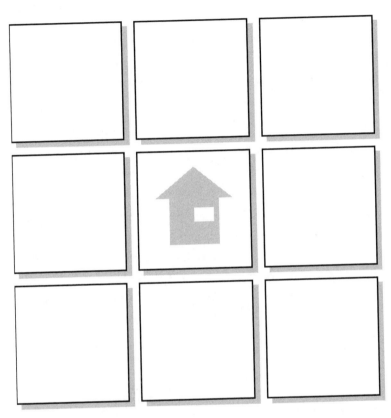

a. Write the names of the people who live in each residence. You may only know first names. Write down what you know.

b. Write down any relevant information about each person that you could only know by having spoken to the person. An example would be, "Grew up in Wisconsin but is a Viking fan who thinks Brett Favre was overrated; grandfather fought in the Battle of the Bulge; speaks three languages."

c. Write down something that's more in-depth. You would only know this information by having had deeper conversations. What are their goals in life? Is there a particular tragedy they have lived through? What do they believe about God, religion, and so on?

Figure 4.1. A neighborhood grid exercise

Loving others begins with seeing them. Loving in abstraction is improbable. This is something Jesus demonstrated over and over. In the encounter with the rich young ruler in which the man asks Jesus what he needs to do to inherit eternal life, the Gospel writer Mark relays the following:

> Jesus looked at him and loved him. "One thing you lack," he said. "Go, sell everything you have and give to the poor, and you will have treasure in heaven. Then come, follow me." (Mk 10:21)

Notice the phrase "looked at him." The original language here is a Greek term used in astronomy. It means something beyond just glancing at or noticing. It means to look at something in order to understand it. Jesus looked at this young man in order to learn about him. And the next words Mark writes are "loved him." Jesus took the time and heart to really see what was inside the young man. This is a lesson for us all. Certainly we should practice such looking wherever we go, but it should start in our neighborhoods.

Seeking the Welfare of My City

The idea of missional church has gained tremendous traction over the last decade. But the most common missteps and misnomers among well-intentioned, rightly motivated leaders happen when the word *missional* is used merely as a fresh term for outreach and evangelism. The difference is this: Missional doesn't visit the neighborhood. It moves into the neighborhood. To be missional is not simply to evangelize; it is to do the hard work of an evangelist— getting to know those who need to hear the message, learning the language and the cultural setting. Missional churches are not necessarily churches that do lots of outreach events. Those programs and activities may emerge, and they should. But what makes a missional church is that it's made up of people who are on missions in their individual lives—their neighborhoods, workplaces and social places—and in their communal activity as a faith collective.

The tendency for most people is to view their neighborhood and city as little more than the place they live. It is a utilitarian place to serve them as they chase their dreams. Most people are hoping for the best: a safe, peaceful, crime-free community, with good schools, parks, employment opportunities and arts and entertainment venues. The missional person sees her neighborhood differently. By the same token, a genuinely missional church views its community differently. It doesn't view its community as a potential market for church growth.

To be missional is not simply to evangelize; it is to do the hard work of an evangelist.

Authentically missional churches consist of people who have individually determined and collectively agreed to own the responsibility for the welfare of their particular community. The realization of any hopes and dreams revolving around missional church weigh in the balance of whether the people of God open their eyes and see their neighborhoods and cities with missionary eyes. This starts with the actual street you and I live on—our most immediate mission field. From this starting point, pathways stretch to our towns, cities and the connecting corridors of residential and commercial happenings.

For close to three decades, I've heard my father-in-law say, "There are givers and takers and other kinds of lovers." Life takes on new meaning when we make conscious and committed decisions—on a daily basis—to seek the best for our neighborhoods and cities. We don't look just to take from our communities. We aim to make our community. One of the passages we frequently open training sessions with is the following:

This is what the LORD Almighty, the God of Israel, says to all those I carried into exile from Jerusalem to Babylon: "Build houses and settle down; plant gardens and eat what they produce. Marry and have sons and daughters; find wives for your sons and give your daughters in marriage, so that they too may have sons and daughters. Increase in number there; do not decrease. Also, seek the peace and prosperity of the city to which I have carried you into exile. Pray to the LORD for it, because if it prospers, you too will prosper." (Jer 29:4-7)

In the Old Testament we see the Lord choose a people for a purpose. That purpose is not to reject the other peoples. Johannes Verkuyl says, "In choosing Israel as segment of all humanity, God never took his eye off the other nations; Israel was the *pars pro toto*, a minority called to serve the majority. God's election of Abraham and Israel concerns the whole world."[2] The same is true of the church. God chose the church to be his instrument of witness to a fallen world—an instrument of love that reaches out with his kindness, joy, compassion and mercy. As God's missionary people— the sent ones—it is incumbent on us to constantly ask missionary questions regarding the neighborhoods we live in, the places we work and the marketplaces we frequent. Some questions we should be asking regarding our neighborhoods:

- How would a missionary live on my street?
- What would he or she notice is missing here?
- Who are the poor, marginalized and hurting in our midst?
- In what ways would my neighborhood be different if God's kingdom came here as it is in heaven?
- What would good news be for my neighbors right here, right now?[3]

Frank Laubach said, "The simple program of Christ for winning the whole world is to make each person he touches magnetic enough with love to draw others."[4] Jesus instructed his followers to manifest

As God's missionary people—the sent ones—it is incumbent on us to constantly ask missionary questions.

faithfulness by shining brightly in tangible ways. Churches are cities on hills, lights in the midst of darkness. People in the surrounding neighborhoods may or may not join these churches, but they should be witnesses to Christians and churches acting as essential components of the health and hope of their communities. Jesus said,

> You are the light of the world. A town built on a hill cannot be hidden. Neither do people light a lamp and put it under a bowl. Instead they put it on its stand, and it gives light to everyone in the house. In the same way, let your light shine before others, that they may see your good deeds and glorify your Father in heaven. (Mt 5:14-16)

Jesus brings up the issue of good works, which can be a bit of a touchy term for some folks. But he is clear on the issue. Good works done in the name of Christ bring glory to God. Now, our efforts in this regard sometimes communicate that doing the deed is more important to us than the person at the receiving end. Good works can easily become dead works if they are not motivated by and delivered in love. A competent and resourceful missions agency can unintentionally communicate that solving a problem is more important than knowing the people with the problem. Government organizations can also be guilty of this. What these types of groups cannot offer is something only another human can do—build meaningful relationships with the people in need.[5] Urban missionary John Hayes writes,

When missionaries start with the need, hoping they will one day get to know poor people personally, they are likely to be found 10 years later, still addressing the need. They are welcome, even necessary, outsiders, but outsiders nonetheless. On the other hand, when mission workers start with poor people in empowering relationships, they are likely to get to the problems, together with the poor. The "work" typically starts slower and looks less impressive when relationship is prioritized before attention to the need, but it is more likely to be owned and reproduced by the poor themselves and, as a result, have a much longer lifespan.[6]

Hayes points out one of the most troubling points for most pastors and ministry leaders. We live in such a microwave culture that results are expected to come about immediately. If farmers had the mindset that most pastors and denominational leaders have, they would dig up the corn seed that doesn't produce stalks within a week. Relationships take time—a lot of time. This is why attempts to be missional without being incarnational most often fail to transform communities.

HIDDEN TREASURE

Every so often stories emerge of rare items or hoards of cash found beneath art canvases, walls or wooden floors and the like. Such a story unfolded recently in Defiance, Ohio. Karl Kissner was sorting through long-forgotten items stored in his late grandfather's attic when from underneath a wooden dollhouse he pulled out a dusty cardboard box. It contained what experts later appraised to be a collection of baseball cards worth up to three million dollars. Kissner's grandfather had placed the cards in the attic at some point and died in the 1940s. It took six decades for it to be discovered. We can only imagine how many attics across our cities hold similar fortunes.

In the same way, every neighborhood has its own hidden treasure. On a recent trip back to my hometown for my thirtieth high school reunion I was on a sentimental journey through my old neighborhood. Keller was now pushing fifty thousand in population and barely resembled its former self. As I was driving into Indian Meadows (a long-forgotten moniker), a collection of misty memories began to unfold, producing a stream of tears down both my cheeks.

I parked in front of my old house for a few minutes and saw visions from years past. There I was, forty years prior, flying my bicycle over rows of metal garbage cans—something all young mid-1970s boys did in imitation of our hero Evel Knievel. My father was in the driveway changing the oil on his '65 Impala while my faithful dog Popcorn lay under the garage eve panting. From next door, Bull and Dorothy Durham strolled across the St. Augustine lawn my mom so lovingly planted and tended to share homemade peach ice cream under the shade of the huge mimosa tree in our front yard. And Don, Janie and their little blonde boys, Andy and Joey, walked across the street to join us.

Gathering my composure, I puttered down the street a couple of blocks when I passed a house that prompted me to laugh out loud. I spotted an older gentleman working in the front flower bed. As I drove on I wondered—could that have been him?

In the mid-1970s Mr. and Mrs. Burks moved into the neighborhood and installed an old church bell atop the courtyard wall of the front porch. This was a standing invitation to adolescent boys. Every so often, late in the evening, my buddies and I would sneak up to the Burkses' front porch and ring that bell, causing every dog on the block to bark like mad and porch lights to flip on up and down the street. We ran like our lives depended on it and hid in the tall Johnson grass in the nearby fields.

Thirty-five years had passed and it was just possible that Mr. Burks was still around. I decided to turn around and find out. As I pulled along the curb parallel to the front yard, the old man was on one knee pulling weeds, his back to the street. I began walking toward him and so as not to startle him, I yelled, "Mr. Burks?" Turning around with a smile, he stood up and said in a high-pitched voice, "Yes, sir. How can I help you?"

As he pulled a glove off to shake my hand, I introduced myself and said, "Mr. Burks, I'm here to confess that I used to ring your bell." He threw back his head and laughed uproariously. He pitched his garden tools onto the ground and said, "Come in— come inside and let's visit." We spent a wonderful hour together, Mr. Burks choking up more than once as he told me how his wife of fifty-nine years had passed away less than three months ago. They were never able to conceive children and his days had become lonely; he was, in fact, filled with grief. I prayed with him and promised to continue to pray for him.

Though Mr. and Mrs. Burks never raised children, it didn't mean they didn't have kids. During our visit Mr. Burks took me out to his workshop where he'd repaired countless flat tires and chains during the last forty years, fixing up the neighborhood children's bikes. He was now playing Mr. Fixit for the children of the kids he'd helped out three decades earlier. He was the neighborhood grandpa. Mr. Burks was and continues to be a neighborhood treasure.

BUILDING A COLLECTIVE

Neighborhood cultivators search for the treasures of skill, aptitude, hospitality and grace that exist in the homes in their communities. In a wonderful book on developing vibrant communities, *The Abundant Community*, Peter Block and John Mc-Knight say, "The tragedy of a dysfunctional family or neighborhood is that the potential gifts of its members are never given."[7] Calling it a tragedy is not an overstatement. To let the readily available treasure of skill, wisdom and knowledge be wasted is grossly poor collective stewardship. In the small group workbook we wrote for people that want to live on mission, *The Missional Essentials*, we point out,

> The Church is not the kingdom of God. It is an instrument, or entity, within the kingdom. It is incumbent upon us, therefore, that we understand who we are and assume the role of servant for the kingdom of God. We are God's tangible expression for how he feels about the world. Most Christians are overwhelmed by—what they believe to be— their own lack of talents, giftings, or expertise to help others. The good news is that none of us must have all the answers, resources, or solutions. That is one of the things that makes community so colorful and creative.[8]

Neighborhoods do not need a hero. No one person need be spectacular. No one person has to have all the answers. It is the collective input of wisdom, talent, skill and support via multiple hands and voices that brings the resources and answers a neighborhood needs to survive, much less thrive. As Block and Mc-Knight put it, "We begin to see that the neighborhood is a treasure chest. By opening the chest and putting the gifts together in many different ways, we multiply the power of its riches."[9]

Think for a moment about the street you live on. Consider the homes on either side of your house as they stretch in both directions. What do you know of the people who live in the houses on the other side of your street? It would amaze us all if we were tuned in to the wide array of gifts and talents of the people living in those homes—not to speak of the resources contained in their garages, sheds and houses themselves. Block and McKnight write,

> A competent community builds on the gifts of its people. It knows that a gift is not a gift until it is given. Before it is given, it is only a beautifully wrapped box in a drawer. It is a capacity held in exile. Gifts need to be named and exchanged, not only to create a competent community, but also to create a functioning family. This is a family that has discovered its capacity to produce for itself, together with a competent community, all that is required for a truly good life, a satisfying life. The tragedy of a dysfunctional family or neighborhood is that the potential gifts of its members are never given.[10]

The missional quest of loving our neighborhoods and cities begins as a treasure hunt. When we are willing to accept the challenge of prayerfully opening our eyes and ears, taking some risks to get to know others and giving ourselves as servants, we can play a significant role in the welfare and renewal of our cities. We begin by excavating neighborhood treasure.

The missional quest of loving our neighborhoods and cities begins as a treasure hunt.

NEIGHBORHOOD MINERS

We all know people who are great at throwing parties. They don't even seem to need a special occasion or holiday to form a get-together. More often than not, they're not the life of the party but the life-givers of the party. Neighborhood cultivators are like that. They may or may not be leaders who stand at the front of the room and act as the voice of the group. Rather they are in the middle of the room, always moving, setting up games and scenarios, gathering food, arranging rooms, serving and introducing people to one another. A party thrower is skilled at and fulfilled by bringing people and components together so that a great time can be had by all.

So imagine a church that cultivates and encourages the idea of "neighborhood miners." Leaders who are trying to lead missional churches and communities would do well to cast a vision that raises up people who purposely dig for the divergent gifts, talents and assets in their particular neighborhood—collecting and connecting neighbors to one another. These "miners" have a common mindset:

- They are not necessarily leaders in the common sense of the word. That is not their identity. But they desire to see their neighborhood become a village and are willing to work to make it happen.

- They believe in the hidden potential of their neighbors. They are not cynics. If they were prospectors of gold rather than neighborhood treasure, they would be the ones yelling, "There's gold in them thar hills!"

- They are connected themselves. They are active in neighborhood activities (if there are any) and are familiar with the personality of their neighborhood.

- They are willing to work. Working a garden is hard work. And cultivating a neighborhood that is most likely gripped by fear and distrust of others, along with a spirit of individualism, means working in hard soil that requires tenaciousness.

One of the great paraphrases of Isaiah 58:12 comes from Eugene Peterson and is a fitting mantra for neighborhood cultivators:

You'll use the old rubble of past lives to build anew,
  rebuild the foundations from out of your past.
You'll be known as those who can fix anything,
  restore old ruins, rebuild and renovate,
    make the community livable again. (Is 58:12 *The Message*)

People on the missional quest are invited to do exactly what this verse describes. We are called to make the community livable. We not only have the invitation—or calling—to do it, we have an obligation as God's missionary people to be driven by this vision. And what fun it is! Who doesn't love a treasure hunt? As we said earlier, quests are driven by questions. Neighborhood miners are constantly asking the same questions of people in the neighborhood and host community:

What is in your mind? On any given street are people who have a wealth of knowledge on a wide range of subjects such as math, science, art, literature, business or even neighborhood history. This knowledge is a rich resource to be tapped into.

What is in your hands? Many people have skills such as musicianship, carpentry, gardening, baking, home maintenance and auto repair. Think of all the tools housed on a typical neighborhood street—gardening, carpentry, mechanical—these are just a few categories that offer an enormous opportunity for sharing and saving on spending.

What is in your heart? Most people are passionate about something. This is about discovering who cares about what in your neighborhood. Some folks are deeply passionate about helping the poor, caring for stray or abused animals, focusing on the needs of children, saving the environment and so on. They may think they are the only one who cares about these things. Helping people who are passionate about certain issues discover one another can be wonderfully catalytic.

Are you willing to teach what you know and share what you have? The first steps in mining the neighborhood involve finding out what's there. The next steps involve finding out what's available. Many people are more than pleased to share their resources.

Who do you know? This is the last question because a neighborhood doesn't know what it needs until it knows what it has. Discovering who knows whom is vital. The adage "It's not what you know but who you know" is good advice. Folks may not be able to do the actual helping themselves, but they often will answer, "I know someone who . . . " Some resources—be they knowledge, information, skill or finances—are beyond the means of the neighborhood itself but not beyond the neighborhood's collective connections. The diverse and vast network connections represented on any given street would most likely surprise us all.

STEPS ON THE QUEST

Consider hosting an event (we suggest an evening with snacks and drinks—keep it fun) focused on the idea of becoming a neighborhood miner. Share the concept. In table groups, have everyone brainstorm the answers to these questions: What is in your mind? What is in your hands? What is in your heart? Are you willing to teach what you know and share what you have? Who do you know?

On a whiteboard or large paper, capture the findings in order to see the riches in your own faith community. Next, issue the challenge for those present to host the same type of event in their homes, inviting their neighbors as participants.

Each year Brad and I lead a training cohort of men and women who desire to learn what it means to live and lead on mission. Those involved include church planters, pastors of existing churches and Christ-followers who are not church staff members but are trying to learn what it means to live on mission. Matt and Stephanie Christenot are a couple from Lawrence, Kansas, who participated in a recent cohort. They began the training as a somewhat last-ditch effort to get their heads around what a missional community in the suburbs of their Midwestern city might look like. Just as we were wrapping up our nine-month learning journey, Matt and Stephanie told us about an experiment they were going to try that involved inviting a couple of experts on community needs to speak at a gathering that they would host in their home. They planned to invite a mixture of friends, both Christian and nonbelievers, to join the gathering. The day after the event we both received the following email from Matt:

> We had twenty adults and fourteen kids in our house last night. There were actually four more who couldn't attend at the last minute as well as a few others who wanted to be there but are out of the country. Out of that thirty-four, I believe we were about a sixty-forty split on believers and nonbelievers. We had two guest speakers, Jeremy Farmer from Just Food, the Douglas County food bank, and Jon Stewart from the Heartland Community Health Center. Both of these guys did an absolutely incredible job explaining what they do and why they do it. They talked about what constitutes poverty and how they advocate for both the physical well-being as well as the dignity of those who are in need. Jeremy talked about the cyclical nature of poverty and how food relates to that. The money quote

from Jon was that we think about poverty in terms of a lack of money, but rarely do we recognize relational poverty.

As I mentioned, this was a very mixed group. Some have done some Bible studies with us and are exploring Jesus, some we have yet to go that far with, and still others were full-on followers of Jesus. Having said that, both Jon and Jeremy come at the issue of justice from a believing perspective and they did not hide that. I watched our friends who don't know Jesus as they were glued to the words of Christ's compassion that were shared by our guests. I began the night by talking about how our dignity stems from being created in the image of God and Jon and Jeremy used several illustrations from the life of Jesus to make their points. Everyone was extremely moved and encouraged.

After the night was over people stayed and talked for over an hour. I looked around the room and saw our friends Rob and Rachel who are doing the [book study] with us conversing with our former neighbors. I was so proud to see them looking like naturals and practicing what we have been learning. Conversations about justice and hospitality were happening all over. Our friends Matt and Kristie, who have done some Bible studies with us, were probing Steph and me on how they could be better at making friends and building networks. Anyway, it was a beautiful night.

Matt and Stephanie's idea to bring in community advocates was strategic. It broke the ice on getting to know people in their neighborhood and was a common-ground rallying point. By inviting some of their current friends, they broke through on the possibility of integrating their longtime friends with their new friends, some of whom are Christians and some who are not-yet-Christians. The same type of event could take place around numerous subjects—community gardening, housing advocacy, youth at risk, art—an entire series could be offered.

PROXIMITY SPACES

To think in missional terms is to think outside of the church box. Every opportunity we can find to intermingle our lives and activity with non-Christ-followers is part of the work of an evangelist. In chapter seven we will cover this idea more thoroughly, but for now let us say that proximity spaces are places or events where Christians and not-yet-Christians join in common experiences or projects. These spaces can run the gamut of art galleries to cafes and pubs, from urban gardens to dog parks. Missiologists Alan Hirsch and Michael Frost write,

> Missional church thinking values the development of shared or joint projects between the Christian community and its host community. Proximity spaces are excellent for casual interaction. Shared projects allow the Christians to partner with unbelievers in useful, intrinsically valuable activities within the community. In the context of that partnership, significant connections can be established. The church can initiate these shared projects though presented as a community-wide activity. Or the Christian community can simply get behind existing projects. The important thing is to find joint projects that put Christians and not-yet-Christians shoulder-to-shoulder in a lengthy partnership. Time is an issue here. We need to find or develop projects that allow the time for important friendships to form.[11]

When Joey Turner led the charge to plant a missional community in the Fairmount neighborhood of urban Fort Worth, Texas, one of the first things his group noticed after moving into the neighborhood was that there were a lot of people with dogs but there was no nearby park for the dogs to run and play. They took it upon themselves to sponsor the first Fairmount Pooch Park Social; a pop-up dog park that brought tons of neighbors together in a local vacant

> *Every opportunity we can find to intermingle our lives and activity with non-Christ-followers is part of the work of an evangelist.*

lot turned doggie central. Local businesses provided food and drink and the event went so well that they followed it up the next month with Yoga In the Park. Neighbors who were strangers before these events have cracked the code on getting to know one another via a simple and practical social event.

The Fields Are Alive

Look at your neighborhood as a vast field. What amending needs to be done? What can grow there right now? What stumps, rocks, weeds and rubbish need to be removed? What would it take to make this collection of housing into a neighborhood of neighbors? Henri Nouwen wrote, "The mystery of the incarnation reveals to us the spiritual dimension of human solidarity. Because all humanity has been taken up into God through the incarnation of the Word, finding the heart of God means finding all the people of God." This is an important impetus for neighborhood cultivators. Being formed in the image of God, every human being living in our neighborhood possesses God-given gifts to be shared with others. Nouwen continues, "We cannot live in intimate communion with Jesus without being sent to our brothers and sisters who belong to that same humanity that Jesus accepted as his own. Thus intimacy manifests itself as solidarity and solidarity as intimacy."[12]

About three years ago my wife and I moved into a historic Kansas City neighborhood with houses built in the early 1900s. One particular neighbor stood out because of his eccentric ways. Sadly, many of the neighbors referred to him as Crazy Stan.[13] A few months after moving into the neighborhood, one afternoon I was able to meet Stan and strike up a conversation. At first he was aloof and stand-offish. His first words were a terse, "What do you want?" After assuring him that I didn't want anything, I ended up having a long, enjoyable visit—finding him to be an absolutely fascinating, well-read and brilliant person who was an early pioneer in the computer sciences field. After almost an hour, I told Stan I needed to get going. Stan said, "I really enjoyed our talk. Thanks for coming over, Lance."

A couple of weeks later Brad came to my house and upon leaving came across Stan, who was struggling to carry a bag of groceries while trying to use his walker. Brad stopped his car, jumped out and offered to help. About an hour later Brad called and said, "I just met Stan. He's amazing!" This was the beginning of a friendship between Stan—labeled a crazy hermit by at-a-distance neighbors—and my family and me. Since then it has become the norm for Stan to share holiday meals and full afternoons and evenings with the Ford household. Block and McKnight speak to all-too-common scenarios such as this:

> While we all have deficiencies and problems, some of our neighbors get labeled by their deficiencies or condition. They are given names like mentally ill, physically disabled, developmentally disabled, youth-at-risk, single mom, welfare recipient, cranky, loner, trailer court person, immigrant, low income. All of these people have gifts we need for a really strong community. And many of them desperately need to be asked to join and contribute. Their only real deficiency is the lack of connection to the rest of us. And our greatest community weakness is the fact that we haven't seen them and felt their loneliness. We have often ignored or even feared them. And yet their gifts are our greatest undiscovered treasure![14]

Sharing resources of heart, hand and mind not only saves money for everyone involved, it more importantly brings people together by spurring and cultivating relationships. It weaves the fabric of community. It also can serve to empower others. Some folks would be shocked to find out how much the people around them desire to tap into their wisdom. Becoming a participant in a connected neighborhood can totally reinvigorate people of all ages, not the least of whom are senior citizens, who too often are oppressed by the tormenting voices that tell them they are useless and not needed by others.

"OUR EARTH" AS IT IS IN HEAVEN

Recently I was chatting with a few others during a break at a conference where I was speaking when one of the guys shared an experience from the previous Sunday in a church where he'd been guest preacher. When the church service was over an elderly lady approached and asked if he would like to hear what had happened in her life in the past year since he had first preached in her church. She reminded him that the year before he had shared a message on God calling everyone to be missionaries in their own neighborhoods and she had approached him, quite distraught. She'd shared that she was an aged widow and too old for God to use her. She wished she would have known about what he was speaking on years before. "You asked me if I would be willing to simply start praying for God's kingdom to come on my neighborhood—my earth—as it is in heaven," she said. "You particularly pointed out that the kingdom of God is good news and that I should ask the Lord to show me what good news would look like in my neighborhood. Wanna know what has happened over the last year?"

He said, "I'm not leaving here until you tell me."

The first evening she had prayed, "Lord, please bring your kingdom here on my earth—to my apartment building. Please bring good news here." Later that evening she began to think about the people who lived near her, few of whom she knew very well. Her complex housed mostly lower-middle- and low-income families, including many single moms and their children. Each school day a handful of teenagers congregated on the front stoop early in the morning, waiting for the school bus. She thought, "I bet some blueberry muffins would be good news to them."

The next morning she haltingly approached the teenagers, offering a pan of warm muffins. The teenagers thanked her and scarfed them down in a flash. She felt so good about the experience that for the next three mornings she did the same thing for the same kids. By Friday of that week something had changed. Ten teenagers were gathered at the stoop. When she walked up with the muffins she heard one of the kids say to another, "See, I told you. Free muffins." Over the next six weeks this widow lady on a fixed income baked muffins for more than a dozen teenagers.

One afternoon the apartment manager paid her a visit to speak with her about what she was doing with the teenagers. She was startled, thinking the management must have felt she was doing something wrong.

"Oh no," the manager said. "Today in our staff meeting we were trying to figure something out. You see, we spend a lot of money every week repairing broken windows, fixing holes in hallway walls, and cleaning graffiti off the building. Over the last month we have not had to fix one thing. We have never had a month with no issues. We couldn't figure it out. The staff began talking about it and we came to the conclusion that your muffins have something to do with it."

He went on to tell her that he knew her finances were very tight and it must be hard for her to buy all those muffins. From now on, he said, "if you will keep making those muffins, your rent is free."

Over the next few months the kids began dropping by after school, and at one point they asked her why she'd started making the muffins. She shared her story about how it started and thus began sharing her faith. Several of these teenagers became Christ-followers. This little old lady developed a substantial relationship with a couple dozen teenagers and their single moms to the point that her church purchased a van for the sole purpose of transporting them back and forth to church. She had become a youth pastor in her seventies in less than a year.

Loving our neighbors begins with knowing who they are and what they do and do not have. The missional quest has everything to do with discovering the answers to questions we have pored over in this chapter. The greatest need in this regard is Christ-followers who are willing to ask the questions and pursue the answers.

5

Home, Work and God's Mission

Engaging Your First and Second Places

Brad Brisco

• • •

*In the cherry blossom's shade
there's no such thing as a stranger.*

KOBAYASHI ISSA

*We always treat guests as angels—
just in case.*

BROTHER JEREMIAH

*I was a stranger and you
welcomed me.*

MATTHEW 25:35 ESV

In the book The Great Good Place, sociologist Ray Oldenburg coins the language of first, second and third places. For Oldenburg, our first place is where we live, our second place is where we work (or the marketplace in general) and our third place is a setting of common ground or "hangout." When referring to these different places, we can simply speak of them as the places we live, work and play. It is important to recognize that God has positioned us in each of these places for a missional purpose.

Before examining each of these specific places from a missional perspective (first and second places in this chapter and third places in the next), let's consider the importance of place in general. This is necessary because within many Christian circles we have accepted a distorted view of earthly place.

There is a hymn from several decades ago called "This World Is Not My Home." The popular refrain emphasizes that our time on this earth is only temporary.

> This world is not my home, I'm just passing through.
> My treasures are laid up somewhere beyond the blue.
> The angels beckon me from Heaven's open door
> And I can't feel at home in this world anymore.[1]

This song exemplifies a prevalent attitude held by Christians today: a belief that sees this world as little more than a holding station or terminal that provides temporary lodging as we await our final destination. In other words, this world is not our ultimate home. Moreover, the places we currently inhabit are fleeting and perishable. This widespread understanding of our existence on this earth holds that we are created for another world—another place.

This view of the world and our place in it is not entirely unexpected. The Bible does describe our standing in this world as that of aliens and sojourners in a foreign land. Furthermore, we know we are created as eternal beings. If we are followers of Jesus, we will spend eternity in heaven.

But what if, without losing any of the reality of our eternal existence, we began to appreciate the fact that this world *is* our home? What if we saw this place—our neighborhood, our city, our world—as a place of eternal significance? How might we care for our surroundings differently if we saw earthly places as a part of the new creation? What if we stopped trying to escape this world and instead were reminded that God has given us care for all of creation, including the places we inhabit and those who inhabit them with us?

The Bible explains that the current creation is groaning as in labor, eagerly awaiting the day when it will give birth to the new (Rom 8:22). The resurrection of Jesus is a foreshadowing of future events. The corruptible will become incorruptible. The old will be transformed into the new. The new creation will not be totally new, but like the risen body of Jesus, it will be fashioned out of the old.[2]

However, instead of conceiving of a re-creation of the world, many Christians view creation in a gnostic kind of way. Heaven is our spiritual home and is good. The world is physical, corrupted by sin, and therefore not good. And because the world is not good, it will one day be destroyed. This sacred-secular divide has done great harm to the way we think about and engage place. It keeps us insulated from the world God loves. Because of fear of the so-called secular, we fail to fully engage certain parts of the created world. By separating the sacred and secular, the physical and spiritual worlds, we have come to believe that driving across town to attend a church (sacred place) in another neighborhood can faithfully express our call to follow

Jesus.[3] We don't even see how we have divorced our call to incarnational mission from God's activity in the "ordinary" or secular places of daily life.

Wendell Berry helps us rethink the sacred-secular divide when he declares, "There are no unsacred places; there are only sacred places and desecrated places."[4] If Berry is correct, then part of what it means to be a follower of Jesus is to "resacralize" the desecrated places. The apostle Paul says we are ambassadors of reconciliation (2 Cor 5:17-19). The ministry of reconciliation should certainly extend to—and perhaps even be rooted in—particular places.

Therefore we must move beyond seeing this world as a meaningless, short-term dwelling as we await our final and more chief destination. Christianity is much more than that. And anyway, is that the kind of Christianity we really want? Is that the type of Christianity the world needs? What good are we to a world full of brokenness, alienation and hopelessness if followers of Jesus are simply waiting with our ticket punched for a trip to another world? If we are just passing through, why should we be concerned about this place?

This kind of attitude, even if not overtly exhibited, provides little motivation for getting our hands dirty in this life. There is no real need to interact with others—to learn who they are, what they struggle with and how we can be ministers of reconciliation. If we are simply sojourners from another land just passing through this one, it's too easy to neglect our immediate surroundings.

That certainly wasn't how Jesus viewed this world. Even though he had a definite destination and he knew where he was going, he didn't treat this world like he was merely passing through. As Richard Soule says, "He stopped to talk to people about their lives and their struggles. He healed their physical and spiritual wounds. He fed them. He challenged them. He taught them. He offered them hope. During his earthly ministry, this world was certainly His home."[5]

What good are we to a world full of brokenness, alienation and hopelessness if followers of Jesus are simply waiting with our ticket punched for a trip to another world?

A couple of summers ago my family took a three-week "historical" road trip from Kansas City to the East Coast. We spent several days in colonial Williamsburg, Philadelphia, Gettysburg, Jamestown, Yorktown and Mount Vernon. We took a total of twenty-two days to not only visit these and other historical sites but to ensure that we had plenty of time to enjoy the trip in its entirety. We deliberately focused on the journey and not just the destinations. We paid close attention to every place along the way. As we entered a new city we took notice of its uniqueness. My wife conducted preliminary research on many of the towns and as we entered a new city she would read to the whole family what made that place special. When was the city founded? What unique stories surrounded its history? What would make the city a great place to live today?

We not only wanted to understand what made a city tick, we also desired to be sensitive to what God might prompt us to see and do while we were there. Before the trip we set aside a certain amount of money for the purpose of blessing others. As we entered a city we would take special care to watch and listen for ways God might be telling us to engage. One evening my youngest son and I walked to a restaurant for ice cream. While standing in line I got an overwhelming feeling that we were supposed to buy dinner for a couple that appeared, at least from the outside, to be in need of some assistance. After placing enough money on their table to more than cover the cost of their dinner and telling them that God had prompted us to buy their meal, my son and I proceeded out the door to walk back to our hotel. We were halfway across the parking lot when we heard a woman's voice shouting behind us. She ran to us, crying profusely. "Why did you do that?" she asked. For fifteen minutes we stood in the parking lot explaining our actions and listening to her story.

Here's the point. As a family, we were sojourners. We were foreigners from another land. We didn't live anywhere near the East Coast. We were not residents of any of the cities we visited. Instead we were from another place. We were passing through. But that didn't keep us from listening, learning and caring about our surroundings. In fact, knowing that we might not make it this way again provoked us to experience and engage on a deeper level.

So it's true that someday this world will not be our home—but today, it is!

FIRST PLACE: WHERE WE LIVE

So now let's return to the discussion on the specific places where we live, work and play. When considering our "first place"—our home—there are at least two primary themes to examine: neighborliness and hospitality. Since we dealt with the importance of knowing and loving our neighbors in chapter four, lets discuss the idea of biblical hospitality.

We use the adjective *biblical* to help differentiate this particular form of hospitality from what usually comes to mind. Most often we imagine that being hospitable revolves around entertaining: inviting family and friends into our homes for a meal or a night of fun and games.

Let's be clear. There's nothing wrong with sharing a meal

with friends and family. In fact, times spent eating together help cultivate healthy family relationships and are an essential element of biblical community. However, conventional entertaining generally focuses on the host—and in doing so it can become a pride issue. As hosts we become concerned about what others will think. How will our home reflect on us? Will our guests like us and the place we live? What if everything's not perfect? If the house isn't spotless and well-decorated, how can we possibly entertain guests? This sort of hospitality holds up a false ideal that's all about making ourselves look good. This "entertaining" form of hospitality can easily be more about appearances than people.

The word *hospitality* might also bring to mind the hospitality industry, which includes hotels, restaurants and cruise ships that work judiciously to create an atmosphere of friendliness and welcome. Or perhaps church hospitality teams come to mind—teams that include greeters, ushers and those who set up coffee and snacks for the Sunday morning gathering. Author Christine Pohl says in one of the best books on hospitality (aptly titled *Making Room*) that in either case, "most understandings of hospitality have a minimal moral component—hospitality is a nice extra if we have the time or the resources, but we rarely view it as a spiritual obligation or as a dynamic expression of vibrant Christianity."[6] The fact is that over time the Christian community has lost touch with the amazing, transformative realities of true biblical hospitality.[7]

But what exactly is biblical hospitality? A good place to start is to consider the meaning of the word in Scripture. In the New Testament, the Greek word for "hospitality" is *philoxenia*, which is a combination of two words: *phileo* (love) and *xenos* (stranger). It literally means "love of stranger." There are several implications to this definition.

First, in order to love the stranger and open our homes effectively, we need to expand our view of hospitality. Jesus challenges us to extend our circle beyond friends and relatives to include those in need:

> When you give a luncheon or dinner, do not invite your friends, your brothers or sisters, your relatives, or your rich neighbors; if you do, they may invite you back and so you will be repaid. (Lk 14:12)

Notice that the practice of genuine, biblical hospitality is distinct from entertaining because it reaches out to those who cannot reciprocate. Jesus tells us to invite those who can't pay us back. In other words, invite those who are in need. Often when we invite friends into our homes for dinner there is an expectation that next time they will return the favor and have us over to their house. But the point of this passage is that customary "payback" hospitality is of no merit to God. As Darrell Bock puts it, "The best hospitality is that which is given, not exchanged."[8]

The practice of genuine, biblical hospitality is distinct from entertaining.

A second important aspect of biblical hospitality is the understanding that strangers are not only people we don't know. In a strict sense, strangers are those who are disconnected from basic relationships. So hospitality is not only about creating physical environments that are welcoming to others; it is also about the posture we take toward human relationships in general.

How many people do we know in our neighborhoods who are living lives severed from basic relationships? Hospitality involves cultivating connections with those disconnected people. It encompasses a willingness to listen well to those who rarely have a voice. It is about turning our lives toward the other, welcoming them into a relationship with us and also inviting them into our network of relationships. Pohl remarks on this broader understanding of hospitality:

> When we offer hospitality to strangers, we welcome them into a place to which we are somehow connected—a space that has meaning and value to us. This is often our home, but it also includes church, community, nation, and various other institutions. In hospitality, the stranger is welcomed into a safe, personal, and comfortable place, a place of respect and acceptance and friendship. Even if only briefly, the stranger is included in a life-giving and life-sustaining network of relations. Such welcome involves attentive listening and mutual sharing of lives and life stories. It requires an openness of heart, a willingness to make one's life visible to others, and a generosity of time and resources.[9]

Here's an example of being included relationally from my own life. During my senior year of high school I worked part time on a large farm just outside of town. During the fall there were so many acres needing to be plowed that for several days tractors would operate late into the evening. Being the youngest worker and the only non-family member, I usually drew the shortest straw and was stuck with the late-night shift.

One evening I didn't finish plowing until around one in the morning. As I drove the tractor back toward the barn I noticed a light still on in the farmhouse. When I reached the barn, Betty, a wonderful Christian wife and mother in that farming family, came out to tell me she'd kept dinner warm and invited me to eat before traveling home. I sat at one end of the large kitchen table enjoying a huge plate of chicken, potatoes, green beans and homemade dinner rolls while Betty asked me questions about my life and family.

I had never had an adult outside of my own family welcome me in such a way. Betty not only opened her home to me, she welcomed me into her family. More than thirty years later I still vividly remember what it felt like to be included. I experienced true biblical hospitality that evening. As a young man who was experiencing the standard feelings of teenage rebellion and confusion, I felt loved, honored and welcomed that night. And I remember, as someone who didn't know Jesus, wondering what on earth made this woman different. Why did she care to know who I was? Why did she want to hear my story? And why was I more than simply a boy who was hired to drive a tractor? In that simple act of hospitality Betty gave me a glimpse into an alternative way of living.

In Elizabeth Newman's definition, hospitality is a practice that "asks us to do what in the world's eyes might seem inconsequential but from the perspective of the gospel is a manifestation of God's kingdom."[10] Looking back I now see that that's exactly what I experienced around that kitchen table that evening: a manifestation of God's kingdom. I was being invited into another family.

Being included is at the core of biblical hospitality. If we had to take all of this talk about loving strangers and welcoming people into our lives and homes and boil it all down into one word, it would be the word *inclusion*. As followers of Jesus we are called to be the most radically inclusive people on earth. The opposite of inclusion is exclusion, which involves dismissal and rejection. Exclusion is not the way of Jesus. Can you remember a time in your life when you were excluded? Stop and think for a moment. How did being excluded from the lives and activities of others make you feel? Being left out—rejected by others—is deeply hurtful.

The sad reality is that many people live a life of constant exclusion. They are not welcomed— by anyone. They are left to fend for themselves at the margins, on the fringes of society. But hospitality, when rightly understood and pursued, has the power to break the bonds of exclusion.

> *Being included is really at the core of biblical hospitality. . . . Exclusion is not the way of Jesus.*

If hospitality is clearly presented in Scripture, and if it gives us the capacity to overcome the relational separation so prevalent today, why don't we practice it? Hospitality was clearly expressed in the early church and throughout much of the history of Christianity, but the church today is not known for radical hospitality toward strangers. After a wonderful historical survey of the tradition of hospitality, including an examination of the words and activities of Jesus, the apostle Paul, John Chrysostom, Martin Luther, John Calvin and others, Christine Pohl writes,

> Even a superficial review of the first seventeen centuries of church history reveals the importance of hospitality to the spread and credibility of the gospel, to transcending national and ethnic distinctions in the church, and to Christian care for the sick, strangers, and pilgrims. Granting that the practice was rarely as good as the rhetoric, still, we pause to wonder, if hospitality to strangers was such an important part of Christian faith and life, how did it virtually disappear?[11]

When did we lose the capacity to give and receive hospitality? Why has it more or less vanished from the life of the church? The reasons are undoubtedly complex, but one of the greatest enemies of hospitality is fear. Daniel Homan and Lonni Collins Pratt put it this way:

> The stranger next door, and at our door, is particularly frightening. We won't dodge the difficult reality of actual danger. People have been hurt by strangers. You need only to turn on the evening news to be aware that we are growing into a fearful people, suspicious of strangers and outsiders. When we speak of the depth of hospitality, we are proposing something scary and radical. But it's worth the risk. Unless we find a way to open ourselves to others, we will grow even more isolated and frightened. If we do not find and practice ways of hospitality we will grow increasingly hostile. Hospitality is the answer to hostility. Jesus said love your neighbor; hospitality is how.[12]

One specific way fear smothers the desire to pursue hospitality is related to our view of the family. Perhaps the greatest barrier to offering our homes to others is how we see the relationship between what takes place inside our homes and what happens outside their walls. The average middle-class American family has increasingly become a place to achieve safety and security from the dangers of secular society. The home has become a stronghold to protect the family from the evils of the world. Writing on the typical American view of the home, Deb Hirsch provides this powerful critique:

> This is "our" space, and those we may "invite" into that space are carefully chosen based on whether they will upset the delicate status quo, inconvenience us, or pose a threat to our perceived safety. In other words, visitors, especially strange ones, stress us out. And while this is in some sense culturally understandable, the negative result

in terms of our spirituality is that the family has effectively become a pernicious idol. . . . Culture has once again trumped our social responsibility. In such a situation, missional hospitality is seen as a threat, not as an opportunity to extend the kingdom; so an idol (a sphere of life dissociated from the claims of God) is born. . . .

It's not hard to see how this is absolutely disastrous from a missional perspective. Our families and our homes should be places where people can experience a foretaste of heaven, where the church is rightly viewed as a community of the redeemed from all walks of life (Revelation 21). Instead, our fears restrict us from letting go of the control and safety we have spent years cultivating.[13]

We often assume that one of our greatest needs in life is safety. But what we really need most is connection with and acceptance from other human beings. Locks and fences can

The home has become a stronghold to protect the family from the evils of the world rather than a place of welcome and hospitality.

never do for our withered souls what friendship and companionship can do. We must recognize that fear is a thief. It will steal our peace of mind and our ability to forge new relationships. Fear will keep us "sealed up in our plastic world with a fragile sense of security. . . . Hospitality is a lively, courageous, and convivial way of living that challenges our compulsion either to turn away or to turn inward and disconnect ourselves from others."[14] Instead we must recognize hospitality as an adventure that takes us to places we never dreamed of going.

My family knows this firsthand. There was a day when we bought into the notion that our home was our castle. It was our personal space that ought not be intruded upon. While we had people in our home on a regular basis, it was almost always at our convenience. We opened our home when the time and circumstances were a good fit for us.

This was true up until a few years ago when we began to rethink the use of our home. After a time of reflecting on the idea of genuine hospitality and recognizing the insanity of maintaining a "home office" that was never used, our family decided to convert that office back into a bedroom to be in a better position to welcome others into our home. We then took the necessary steps to become a foster family. In the first year of providing emergency care for children at risk we had more than forty different kids come through our home—some for only a few days, while others lived with us for several weeks.

We discovered the adventurous nature of hospitality. But beyond that we learned how God uses hospitality to shape and form us. It is impossible to fully articulate how our family has been blessed through this journey. That's the funny thing about biblical hospitality: Just when you think it's about welcoming strangers for their benefit, you realize that it's you being blessed by their presence.

We have learned that hospitality is a spiritual discipline and a missional practice. Both the blessings and difficulties of hospitality are discovered only as hospitality is pursued. The book *Radical Hospitality* contains a line that continues to haunt me: "The real question is not how dangerous that stranger is. The real question is how dangerous will I become if I don't learn to be more open?"[15]

Over the past couple of years I have grown to better understand that statement. Having these children in our home has opened up my life in surprising ways. I look at the kids in our neighborhood differently. I look at children at the store differently.

I see fear and brokenness in their lives that I didn't see before.

It has also forced me to face my own selfishness. There are some days we receive a call to take in a child who desperately needs a safe place—and I hesitate. For a moment I think of all the "important" things I have to do. How might this new addition to our family affect my plans? In what ways might he or she upset the status quo? Then I'm reminded of the healing touch of hospitality. I remember how God has offered hospitality to me. I was once far away, but now I am brought near. I was once a stranger, but now I am a member of God's household (Eph 2).

WHERE DO WE GO FROM HERE?

After coming to grips with the nature and necessity of biblical hospitality, we must realize that the initiation of hospitality is our responsibility as followers of Jesus. In other words, the responsibility for offering hospitality to those who are experiencing estrangement is on us.

In Romans 12:13, most English translations render the apostle Paul's imperative as "practice hospitality." Theologian John Stott, however, says a better translation of "practice" would be the word "pursue." The Christians in Rome were not to simply "practice" hospitality but were instead to "seek out" or "actively look for" opportunities to welcome strangers into their homes and lives. To help drive home his point Stott quotes the early Christian scholar Origen:

> We are not just to receive the stranger when he comes to us, but actually to enquire after, and look carefully for, strangers, to pursue them and search them out everywhere, lest perchance somewhere they may sit in the streets or lie without a roof over their heads.[16]

This is a powerful reminder that the obligation of welcoming the stranger is ours. We need to be proactive in creating places of hospitality. We must constantly be looking for ways to offer hospitality individually as well as collectively as the church. We need to ask, how can we make a place for hospitality in our lives, homes, churches and communities? What are the characteristics of hospitable space? What needs to change in our current situation to pursue hospitality?

To make this a reality we will likely need to reorder things in our lives to meet the necessary demands. Three practical requirements come to mind.

1. Biblical hospitality requires margin. If we are to be in the position to regularly welcome people into our lives, there must be margins in our daily schedules that allow the space for others to enter. We need to literally make room in the hours of our day and the days of our weeks. Hospitality cannot simply be added to already overburdened lives.

Hospitality cannot simply be added to already overburdened lives.

But making room also relates to living space. We should take inventory of our homes and church facilities to identify suitable space to welcome others to live with us. It is impossible to foster a hospitable life without the room—in both time and space—to welcome the stranger. Christine Pohl writes,

> The practice of hospitality forces abstract commitments to loving the neighbor, stranger, and enemy into practical and personal expressions of respect and care for actual neighbors, strangers, and enemies. . . . Claims of loving all humankind, of welcoming "the other," have to be accompanied by the hard work of actually welcoming a human being into a real place.[17]

2. Biblical hospitality requires generosity. Having created the margins to welcome the stranger into our lives we will next need to be willing to give. Living a hospitable life means being generous with everything we own. We come to the realization that God has blessed us for the purpose of blessing others. We give of our material possessions, but we also give when the need is presented to us. Whether that involve food, drink, clothes or a simple welcome—to the least of these.

> "For I was hungry and you gave me food, I was thirsty and you gave me drink, I was a stranger and you welcomed me, I was naked and you clothed me, I was sick and you visited me, I was in prison and you came to me." Then the righteous will answer him, saying, "Lord, when did we see you hungry and feed you, or thirsty and give you drink? And when did we see you a stranger and welcome you, or naked and clothe you? And when did we see you sick or in prison and visit you?" And the King will answer them, "Truly, I say to you, as you did it to one of the least of these my brothers, you did it to me." (Mt 25:35-40 ESV)

3. Biblical hospitality requires sacrifice. It seems that much of the American way is about finding the easy answer. Too many people look for the path of least resistance. We wish that didn't hold true within the church today. But it is true there as well. We look for easy answers to grow the church, for spiritual maturity and for raising our children. Hospitality is not an easy answer. It requires sacrifice. It demands that we chance and change. It always involves risk and the possibility of failure, but as we mentioned earlier, in not pursuing hospitality there is a greater risk that we become less open and more isolated toward the world.

To close out this section on the importance of engaging our first place, one final quote from Christine Pohl:

Hospitality is not so much a task as a way of living our lives and of sharing ourselves. For most practitioners, offering hospitality grows out of their attempt to be faithful to God, to hear God's voice in the Scriptures and in the people around them. They have learned hospitality as they have opened their lives to situations where they could encounter strangers. Gradually, hospitality has become for them both a disposition and a habit. While rarely without difficulty, hospitality can become so fully integrated into who we are and how we respond to others that we cannot imagine acceptable alternative responses.[18]

STEPS ON THE QUEST

Challenge people to identify the strangers in their neighborhood. Are there individuals or groups that are being excluded? Who in the community is without a voice? What people groups need to be included into the life of the church?

Ask your congregation to think "outside the box" when it comes to identifying those in need of hospitality. There may be those such as homeless people, refugees and people with severe disabilities who require a broader church community approach because of the level of need. However, there are many other strangers or neighbors to whom an individual or a single family could offer the gift of hospitality. These groups might include college students, foreign workers, soldiers far away from home, elderly neighbors, families that have recently relocated or persons recovering from an illness.

STEPS ON THE QUEST

How would a biblical understanding of hospitality impact your worship gatherings? How might it change the way you welcome people into church activities? Again, author Christine Pohl states that hospitality can influence our corporate gatherings when she writes,

> *In hospitality, the stranger is welcomed into a safe, personal, and comfortable place, a place of respect and acceptance and friendship. Even if only briefly, the stranger is included in a life-giving and life-sustaining network of relations. Such welcome involves attentive listening and a mutual sharing of lives and life stories. It requires an openness of heart, a willingness to make one's life visible to others, and a generosity of time and resources.[19]*

SECOND PLACE: WHERE WE WORK

When Oldenburg refers to "second places" he is pointing to the places people work. These are typically the settings in which we spend the second-greatest number of hours in our day. In regard to living out of a missional posture, there are two key considerations to the concept of second places.

First, it is important that Christians in the church have a proper understanding of the interplay between faith and work. The language of "vocation" has become a helpful lens through which to view the Christian life and work in relation to God's activity in the world.

The word *vocation* literally means calling. Before Martin Luther and the Protestant Reformation, the word typically referred to a special calling to religious life as a priest, nun or monk. Such a vocation was understood as a higher calling compared with life as a merchant or peasant. Luther rejected this "division between sacred and secular spheres on which the medieval church's understanding of calling was predicated."[20] In so doing, he "broadened the concept of vocation from a very narrow ecclesiastical focus to describe the life and work of all Christians in response to God's call."[21] Therefore it can be said that the doctrine of the priesthood of all believers did not make everyone into church workers; rather, "it turned every kind of work into a sacred calling."[22] Bottom line—all work matters!

When attempting to lead a congregation in a missional direction it will be necessary to help some people reconsider their work. Unfortunately, many Christians see their work as nothing more than a necessary evil. They don't understand how their "ordinary" everyday life is part of the mission of God. In the book *The Mission of God's People* Christopher Wright states,

> God, it would seem, cares about the church and its affairs, about missions and missionaries, about getting people to heaven, but not about how society and its public places are conducted on earth. The result of such dichotomized thinking is an equally dichotomized Christian life. In fact it is a dichotomy that gives many Christians a great deal of inner discomfort caused by the glaring disconnect between what they think God most wants and what they most have to do. Many of us invest most of the available time that matters (our working lives) in a place and a task that we have been led to believe does not really matter much to God—the so-called

secular world of work—while struggling to find opportunities to give some leftover time to the only thing we are told does matter to God—evangelism.[23]

Building on the idea that all work is a sacred calling, the second key aspect of understanding second places is to realize that God is active in our workplaces. As Christians we need to see that our work is not primarily about economic exchange. It is not about getting paid. It is not about climbing the corporate ladder. It is not about achieving the American dream. Instead it is about contributing to and participating in God's mission. Our work, regardless of whether we're paid for it or not, is about our contribution to and participation in God's ongoing mission and activity in the world.

In a fascinating angle on vocation, Luther says that vocation is a mask of God. That is, God hides himself in the workplace:

> To speak of God being hidden is a way of describing His presence, as when a child hiding in the room is there, just not seen. To realize that the mundane activities that take up most of our lives—going to work, taking the kids to soccer practice, picking up a few things at the store, going to church—are hiding places for God can be revelation in itself. Most people seek God in mystical experiences, spectacular miracles, and extraordinary acts they have to do. To find Him in vocation brings Him, literally, down to earth, makes us see how close He really is to us, and transfigures everyday life.[24]

So we look for God in the ordinary, in the sometimes commonplace, day-to-day activity of our work. And we ask questions similar to those already posed in earlier chapters. What does it look like to be a good neighbor—in the workplace?

What does it mean to extend hospitality—to our fellow workers?
God has placed us where we are for a purpose. So we must discover what God is up to and discern how he wants us to participate in what he is doing. In the next chapter we will examine
the final "place" that we should live missionally, and we will
explain why it is of the utmost importance to lean into the lives
of others in each of our first, second and third places.

6

Where Everybody Knows Your Name

The Importance of Third Places

Brad Brisco

● ● ●

Place gathers stories, relationships, memories.

EUGENE PETERSON

Whatever is true for space and time, this much is true for place:
we are immersed in it and could not do without it.
To be at all—to exist in any way—is to be somewhere,
and to be somewhere is to be in some kind of place.

EDWARD CASEY

What suburbia cries for are the means for people to gather easily,
inexpensively, regularly, and pleasurably—a "place on the corner,"
real life alternatives to television, easy escapes from the
cabin fever of marriage and family life that do not
necessitate getting into an automobile.

RAY OLDENBURG

In the late eighties and early nineties, one of the most popular shows on American television was *Cheers,* which was set in a bar in the heart of Boston. The most iconic scene in every episode took place when one particular regular would burst through the front door and everyone would shout his name in unison: "Norm!" The tagline for the show was, "Where everybody knows your name."

The atmosphere within Cheers provides a perfect picture of a cultural phenomenon referred to as a "third place," a phrase coined by sociologist Ray Oldenburg in his 1989 book, *The Great Good Place.* The subtitle of the book provides further explanation: *Cafes, Coffee Shops, Community Centers, Beauty Parlors, General Stores, Bars, Hangouts, and How They Get You Through the Day.*

But how are we to understand third places beyond this helpful list? And why are they an important piece of the missional conversation? In the most basic sense, a third place is a public setting that hosts regular, voluntary and informal gatherings of people. It is a place to relax. It is a place where people enjoy visiting. Third places provide the opportunity to know and be known. They are places where people like to "hang out."

Oldenburg identifies eight key characteristics that conventional third places share:[1]

- *They are neutral ground.* People are free to come and go as they please. No one person is required to play host. Everyone feels at home. There are no time requirements or invitations needed. Much of the time lived in first places (home) and second places (work) is structured, but not so in third places.

- *They act as a leveler.* Third places are inclusive. They are accessible to the general public. People from all walks of life gather there. There are no social or economic status barriers. While individuals tend to select associates and friends from among those closet to them in social rank, third places expand possibilities instead of narrowing them. Worldly status claims must be checked at the door of third places. Oldenburg writes, "The surrender of outward status, or leveling, that transforms those who own delivery trucks and those who drive them into equals is rewarded by acceptance on more humane and less transitory grounds."[2]

- *Conversation is the main activity.* Nothing more clearly indicates a third place than that the talk is lively, stimulating, colorful and engaging. Unlike corporate settings where status often dictates who may speak, when and for how long, third places provide the environment for every voice to be heard.

- *They are accessible and accommodating.* The best third places are those to which one may go at almost any time of day or night with assurance that acquaintances will be there. They tend to be conveniently located, often within walking distance of one's home.

- *There are regulars.* What attracts regular visitors to a third place is not so much the establishment but fellow customers. It is the regulars who give the third place its character and appeal. The regulars set the tone of conviviality. And while it is easy to recognize who the regulars are, newcomers are welcomed into the group.

- *They are low-profile.* As physical structures they are typically plain and unimpressive. They are not elegant. They are not usually advertised. In most cases they are located in older buildings, partly because newer places tend to emerge in prime retail locations that come with expectations of high-volume customer traffic. This runs contrary to the essential need to linger. People share conversation and life with one another while they are "hanging out."

- *The mood is playful.* With food, drink, games and conversation present, the mood is light and playful. Joy and acceptance rule over anxiety and alienation. The mood encourages people to stay longer and to come back repeatedly.

- *They are a home away from home.* At their core they are places where people feel at home. People feel like they belong there and typically have a sense of ownership.

With these characteristics in mind, we can summarize that third places are core settings of informal public life. The term can be used to designate a wide variety of public places that host the "regular, voluntary, informal, and happily anticipated gatherings of individuals beyond the realms of home and work."[3]

Now, you may be asking what these informal gathering places have to do with moving a church in a missional direction. Why is it important for Christ-followers to understand the concept of third places? Because for the most part these places of informal gathering are no longer prominent or plentiful in American communities.

After World War II millions of returning veterans prompted the creation of new developments made up of single-family homes. While life in the subdivision may have "satisfied the combat veteran's longing for a safe, orderly, and quiet haven," it rarely offered the "sense of place and belonging that had rooted his parents and grandparents. . . . And the typical subdivision proved hostile to the emergence of any structure of space utilization beyond the uniform houses and streets that characterized it."[4] There was a near total absence of an informal public life in the construction of these new suburbs. The familiar gathering places of old—the grain elevators, rural co-ops, soda fountains, general stores—had no coun-terparts. Opportunities for community life had simply not been included.

This loss of public life, specifically the decline of third places, has contributed to an epidemic of isolation and loneliness. The majority of people in the United States are living relationally im-poverished lives. There is not enough public space for them to build genuine community and put down roots. And even if there were, the absence of a public life for so long has left many people devoid of the capacity to even know how to cultivate one.

The decline of social connec-tions and the rise of relational iso-lation have been addressed in several books over the past two decades.[5] One of the more com-prehensive surveys on the topic

The majority of people in the United States are living relationally impoverished lives.

can be found in Robert Putnam's *Bowling Alone*. The book details our society's massive decline in social capital, or social relationships and networks of those relationships within a community. In simple terms, social capital is about the quantity and quality of our relationships. The title of the book comes from the fact that while the number of people who bowl has increased in the last twenty years, the number of people who bowl in leagues has actually decreased. In other words, more people are bowling—alone.

Putnam illustrates this decline in a number of areas. He writes of the drop-off in participation in organizations such as the PTA and Lions Club. He discusses the decrease in work-place connections (second places), political involvement, reli-gious participation and simple, informal relational connections. In one very telling example, he writes on the rise of card games in the post-World War II United States.

Although poker and gin rummy were popular, the biggest boom was in bridge, a four-handed game that had become extremely popular by the 1950s. By 1958, according to the most modest estimate, thirty-five million Americans—nearly one-third of all adults—were bridge players. Millions of Americans, both men and women, belonged to regular card clubs—in fact, one of the earliest scientific surveys of social involvement found that in 1961 nearly one in every five adults was a member of a regular foursome. . . . The primary attraction of bridge and other card games was that they were highly social patterns. "Mixed doubles" clubs were, in that more gendered world, one of the most important sites for men and women to gather informally. The rules encouraged conversation about topics other than the game itself, since "table talk" about the state of play was generally frowned on.[6]

Let that sink in for a moment. Just a few decades ago, nearly one-third of the families in the United States would spend one evening a week at the home of another family visiting and playing games. Today, while there are substitutes for card games such as computer and video games and hundreds of television choices, the reality is that those activities are usually done alone.

The deterioration of social connections in our communities should drive us to action. As followers of Jesus we know that we were created as relational beings. We know that God designed us to be in a deep, abiding relationship with him. But we also understand that we were created to be in life-giving relationships with one another. The thought of millions of lonely people sitting at home, languishing relationally from lack of basic human connection should inspire us to bring about change.

But what are we to do? Let us suggest three things in regard to third places.

IDENTIFY AND ENGAGE THIRD PLACES

Third places offer a unique opportunity for missionally minded people to do life in the proximity of others. And while it is true that third places are no longer plentiful, they do still exist. So we first have to find them.

We need to ask, where do people gather to spend time with others? Where are the coffeehouses, cafes, pubs and other hangouts? In some settings these

> *We were created to be in life-giving relationships with one another. . . . Third places offer a unique opportunity for missionally minded people to do life in proximity to others.*

places will be obvious. However, in other neighborhoods you might need to work at identifying these gathering spots.

In addition to the typical third places described by Oldenburg, what are some atypical places where people congregate? Consider locations such as libraries, parks, farmer's markets and workout centers. Once we've identified our third places, we must seek to engage them. As discussed in chapter one, this will involve embedding our lives incarnationally into third places. Ultimately we move from visitor to regular—listening and learning where God is at work and asking how we can participate in what he's doing.

Anytime I frequent a coffee shop I try to be sensitive to the surroundings. Simple things like getting to know the baristas, noting familiar regulars and listening to the conversations taking place are all ways of pressing into the setting. One recent example involved a lively dialogue I overheard at a table just behind where I was sitting. Three people were having a discussion on the Bible and Christian denominations that focused on two primary themes. The first dealt with their belief that the existence of multiple Bible translations proved that the Bible couldn't be trusted. Second, the existence of numerous denominations proved that no one had the answers to spirituality. After listening to the conversation for several minutes, I turned to the group and asked if they would allow me to respond to their questions. They enthusiastically welcomed me to their table to join the discussion.

It's important to recognize that the conversation I had that day in the coffee shop was never going to take place around a church activity. The misconceptions that each of the people in the group had about Jesus, the church and the Bible simply wouldn't allow it to happen. While they were very open to having a thoughtful conversation about spiritual issues, they were not open to that conversation taking place in a church building.

For my wife, an atypical third place is the local Target. A retail store may not be what you'd think of as a gathering place or hangout, but because my wife is intentional and sensitive toward those who work there, as well as fellow shoppers, it becomes a place to provide—even for a short time—significant relational connections. One perfect example involves an elderly woman named Barbara who worked at Target as a food sampler. Over several weeks my wife built a relationship with Barbara. Every time she shopped at Target she made a special effort to find Barbara and cultivate the relationship. I remember the first time I met Barbara she told me that my wife was her angel. The relationship has led to many opportunities to speak into Barbara's life outside her workplace, all because my wife has eyes to see the relational need in the lives of others in public places.

STEPS ON THE QUEST

Challenge each member of your congregation to identify at least three typical third places in their community and three atypical third places. Pick one third place to enter and spend an hour observing. Take note of conversations. What do you notice about people? What is the vibe of the place? How does this third place bring life and vitality to the community? Where do you see or hear God at work in the conversations? How might you join God in this place? This exercise could be practiced through small groups or Sunday school classes.

CREATE ENVIRONMENTS FOR THIRD PLACES TO FLOURISH

In addition to identifying third places that already exist, we also need to create third places where informal meeting space does not exist. On one end of the spectrum this might mean we open a coffee shop, café or bookstore in our neighborhood. This is of course no small undertaking, but even so there are missionally minded Christians across the country who are committing to the creation of third places. Just in the past few months two very different but equally significant coffee shops have been opened in my city for the purpose of creating a third place.

Quay is a coffee shop located in an artsy area of downtown Kansas City started by two church planters, Cory Stipp and Tanner Stevens. These men have both understood the importance of moving into a community with a posture of service toward the neighborhood. Before even considering starting any type of church activity, they created a third place that not only provides space for people to meet but also acts as a vehicle to give back to the community. The proceeds from the coffee shop are used to support neighborhood services and ministries. Cory and Tanner say people were skeptical initially—especially the gay community—of anything that smelled of religion. But with a genuine desire to love and serve, they are beginning to win over the locals.

Located in a bedroom community of less than twenty thousand people outside of Kansas City is another coffee shop called Groundhouse. While the setting is very different from urban Kansas City, the owners, Steve and Beth Hines, also recognized the need to create a space that would bring relational vitality to the community. They have dozens of stories of how Groundhouse has become the gathering place for business people, friends and families.

However, as vital as it is to create elaborate new ventures that function as third places, it's also good to consider simpler approaches. You might create a third place opportunity on your street by operating a nightly fire pit on the driveway. Or perhaps you could host a weekly cookout that encourages neighbors to not only bring food to throw on the grill but lawn chairs for lingering well after the meal is complete. It is simply about creating sweet spots for people to connect.

Our home has a large side yard that acts as a playground for the neighborhood kids. Almost every afternoon there is some kind of team game taking place in the yard. An extra refrigerator in our garage is stocked with juice boxes and popsicles. And in between games the garage becomes a quasi third place. Remember that our homes should be places of welcome. Opportunities to practice biblical hospitality. Places where others like to hang out. Sometimes we may need to be creative in how we think about common spaces in our neighborhoods and how they may enhance relational connections. But it is we who need to create the environments where third places flourish.

SUPPORT AND DEFEND THIRD PLACES

This may sound unusual, but in some cases we need to become city planning advocates because we understand the importance of place for the health and vitality of our communities. Therefore, when there are plans proposed for such things as parks, sidewalks, walking paths, libraries and anything else that would enhance the opportunity for a richer public life, we need to support those plans.

Some suggest that we have lost half of the casual gathering places that existed at midcentury. Oldenburg writes, "Old neighborhoods and their cafés, taverns, and corner stores have fallen to urban renewal, freeway expansion, and planning that discounts the importance of congenial and unified residential areas."[7]

However, some developers are beginning to realize that we are not meant to live this way. They are starting to understand that suburban sprawl has created social isolation that damages society. Others are recognizing that the traditional suburban planning approach is missing the homebuying market. Today only about twenty-five percent of homebuyers fit the traditional "married with children" demographic. So developers are seeing— primarily for financial reasons—that the way they've built out suburban areas has become increasingly irrelevant to the majority of American households. As a result they are beginning to move toward a more integrated model that attempts to weave together space that includes home, retail and public life.

Another improvement in city planning efforts involves a movement referred to as "placemaking," a multifaceted approach to the planning, design and management of public spaces. What's most exciting about the idea of placemaking is the emphasis it puts on the local community's assets and potential to create public spaces that promote health, happiness and well-being. The process of placemaking starts with the real community stakeholders—those who live, work and play in a place. Advocates make a strong case that a "collaborative community process that pays attention to issues on the small scale is the best approach in creating and revitalizing public spaces."[8] What makes a good place great?

It really comes down to offering a variety of things to do in one spot—making a place more than the sum of its parts. A park is good. A park with a fountain, playground, and popcorn vendor is better. A library across the street is even better, more so if they feature storytelling hours for kids and exhibits on local history. If there's a sidewalk café nearby, a bus stop, a bike trail, and an ice cream parlor, then you have what most people would consider a great place.

What if a neighborhood had 10 places that were that good? The area would then achieve a critical mass—a series of destinations where residents and tourists alike would become immersed in the life of the city for days at a time. Taking the next step, what if a city could boast 10 such neighborhoods? Then every resident would have access to outstanding public spaces within walking distance of their homes. That's the sort of goal we need to set for all cities if we are serious about enhancing and revitalizing urban life.[9]

Two things to keep in mind: First, our efforts in the service of things like placemaking and the creation of third places must flow out of our desire to see those who are relationally disconnected become drawn into life-giving relationships with others—and, of course, ultimately with the giver of life. And in those neighborhoods void of healthy places where people can connect relationally with others, we believe the church is required to become the community advocate. Second, our efforts should flow out of the recognition that as an increasing number of people are less interested in the activities of the church, it is we, the missionary people of God, who are sent to engage people in other settings. We are called to be people who love our neighbors—on our street, where we work and in third places.

Let us close this chapter on third places with a story and a challenge from the conclusion of *The Great Good Place*. While to our knowledge Oldenburg is not a follower of Jesus, he has a vision for a better "place" that we believe should burn in the heart of every Christian as we strive to love our neighbors. He tells the story of speaking to an audience on the vanishing of informal public life in the United States.

We are called to be people who love our neighbors— on our street, where we work and in third places.

> I asked the group if Americans living in the suburbs had the freedom to put on their sweaters in the early evening and visit their friends at the neighborhood tavern. A resounding yes was given by the group. I asked if the younger children could go with coins in hand to the corner store and pick out some candy or a comic book. Another resounding yes. Finally, I asked if the older children could stop in at the malt shop after school. Yes was the response of the audience. . . . I'd hoped someone would realize that none of these people can go to a place that isn't there or have an experience that is no longer possible.
>
> The environment in which we live out our lives is not a cafeteria containing an endless variety of passively arrayed settings and experiences. It is an active, dictatorial force that adds experiences or subtracts them according to the way it has been shaped. When Americans begin to grasp that lesson, the path to the planners' offices will be more

heavily trod than the path to the psychiatrists' couches. And when that lesson is learned, community may again be possible and celebrated each day in a rich new spawning of third places. If there is one message I wish to leave with those who despair of suburbia's lifeless streets, of the plastic places along our "strips," or of the congested and inhospitable mess that is "downtown," it is: It doesn't have to be like this![10]

7

Launching Pads

Small Groups Becoming Missional Communities

Lance Ford

• • •

*Our relationship with each other is the criterion the
world uses to judge whether our message is truthful.
Christian community is the final apologetic.*

Francis Schaeffer

*You are the light of the world.
A town built on a hill cannot be hidden.
Neither do people light a lamp and put it under a bowl.
Instead they put it on its stand, and it gives light to everyone in
the house. In the same way, let your light shine before others,
that they may see your good deeds and
glorify your Father in heaven.*

Matthew 5:14-16

For Westerners, individualism is melded into our makeup. It has become the lens through which we see most of life. Try as we might, it is hard for us to shed our individualistic armor and become one with others the way we see lived out in the early church as shown in the New Testament. In the book *Missional Church,* the authors say:

> When the Holy Spirit transforms the life and practice of Christian communities, they demonstrate that God's promised future has been set in motion. The joy, freedom, and wholeness of life within the reign of God can already be tasted even if not yet fully consummated. While not perfection, life within the Christian community reflects, embodies, and witnesses to a "divine infection."[1]

Paul chose the "body of Christ" metaphor in his letters to the churches to emphasize the communal, flesh and blood reality that is the tangible presence of Jesus when the people of God join in covenantal relationship. This manifestation does not take place just because a group of Christians shows up for an hour or so in the same facility each week. No. It is the joined believers, not the gathered ones, who manifest the body of Christ:

> We will grow to become in every respect the mature body of him who is the head, that is, Christ. From him the whole body, joined and held together by every supporting ligament, grows and builds itself up in love, as each part does its work. (Eph 4:15-16)

Notice the phrase "joined and held together . . . as each part does its work." Without a doubt there is a mystical aspect of joining here—the work that only God can do. But there is also the part that we humans must purposefully and actively undertake. We must do our part. Churches can congregate in impressive masses while never becoming a functioning body that manifests the body of Christ to the watching world. In much the same way, small groups can gather consistently, study the Bible, sing worship songs and pray together while failing to join their lives together for the sake of being a missional community. Our friends Michael Frost and Alan Hirsch speak to this issue:

> After giving a seminar on the future shape of the church, Michael went to dinner with some young men. At one point someone said, "I agree with you about the church. It needs a complete overhaul. I mean here we are, six guys eating together, talking about Jesus. We're a church now!" It's tempting, in our efforts to strip back the church from the empire created by Christendom, to overdo it and end up with the belief that any old bunch of believers sitting together in the same room is a church. But the six of us sitting around that table that night were not a church. We had made no mutual commitments, shared no long-term calling, were completely unaccountable to one another, and our purpose for gathering was mainly social. Of course, as Christians, our conversation centered on Christian things, and by the end of the evening we were encouraged in our faith and individual callings. We were doing some of the things a church might do, but our involvement was not permanent.[2]

What Frost describes in his gathering is a bit less than what most small groups do, but it is not far behind. Missional communities are more than small groups that gather to study mission. Mutual commitment, accountability and devotion to one another set them apart as markedly different from the small groups we have settled for in the past. A good picture of the rhythm of the early believers is found in the book of Acts:

They devoted themselves to the apostles' teaching and to fellowship, to the breaking of bread and to prayer. Everyone was filled with awe at the many wonders and signs performed by the apostles. All the believers were together and had everything in common. They sold property and possessions to give to anyone who had need. Every day they continued to meet together in the temple courts. They broke bread in their homes and ate together with glad and sincere hearts. (Acts 2:42-46)

We believe there are three primary relationships evident in this passage and throughout the epistles. The early believers were committed to God, one another and the immediate world around them. The rhythm of their lives was a dance of loving commitment in all three spheres. Several noted thinkers and authors agree that these three commitments exist. Over the years they have given different labels to the three. The late John Wimber, shaper of the Vineyard Association of Churches, called them The Father, The Family and The Field. Mike Breen uses the language of Up, In and Out. Frost and Hirsch speak of Communion, Community and Commission. Regardless of terminology it is important that we nurture our walk with the Lord with a conscious awareness of all three areas.

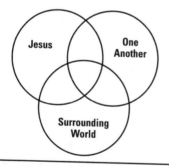

Figure 7.1. Christ-followers' commitments

It is helpful to look at each sphere as an aspect of our relationship with the Lord. First, we have a relationship with Jesus cultivated in prayer, Bible reading, spiritual disciplines and the like. A lot of people hearken to the evangelical tradition, calling this a "personal relationship with

Christ." Developing a hearing ear that is tuned to the voice of God is essential for faithfulness to the call of discipleship. Jesus teaches that abiding in him is the key to fruitfulness (Jn 15).

But a mere personal relationship with Jesus is neither complete nor healthy. A second aspect of our relationship with Jesus is our relationship with the body of Christ. If our relationships are not healthy with other believers then our relationship is not good with Jesus. After all, the church is the body of Christ, the closest flesh and blood manifestation we experience with Jesus this side of the second coming of Christ. The third way we experience relationship with Christ is as he shows up in "the least of these" (Mt 25:31-46). Jesus says the way we treat others in the world around us is the way we treat him. He is personalized in the faces and lives of those in our surrounding community.

STEPS ON THE QUEST

Take the time to evaluate these three areas in your own life. What does the rhythm of your life look like in a typical week? Are you engaging in relationship with Jesus personally, in the body and in the least of these? You may find it helpful to use a calendar to audit your life in these areas for a few weeks.

Missional communities are groups of people who commit to living their lives with devotion of heart, mind, soul and strength in these three spheres of relationship with the Lord. It takes us from the abstract to the concrete—a rubber meets the road Christianity.

PREPARING FOR LAUNCH

I have to admit that I am old enough to remember gathering around my family's washing-machine-sized television set watching history unfold as the Apollo 11 rocket took off on July 16, 1969. Four days later Neil Armstrong was the first human to step foot on the surface of the moon. The lunar mission had been set in motion eight years earlier when President John F. Kennedy declared, "We choose to go to the moon." The mission began from Kennedy Space Center's Launch Complex 39A, where final processing and preparation for takeoff took place.

Rockets are built and maintained away from the launch pad, but the launch pad is where all final preparations take place as the mission team takes care of last-minute tasks. Everything from fuel supply to emergency abort protocol and egress is set in order. Last-minute system checks take place and communication links are connected. Rockets need stability between the time of ignition and engine thrust buildup as they begin to leave the earth's surface, and the launch pad tower provides this guidance. Without the launch pad, the mission would never get off the ground.

The launch pad is a helpful metaphor for small groups that want to become missional communities. Just as the launch pad is not the mission, small groups are not the mission, though they are essential to its success. But too often small groups become an end in themselves. Bible study, fellowship, prayer and so on are seen as the purpose of the group, and while every one of those exercises plays an essential role in the ultimate purpose, they are not why we gather. The reason for missional small groups to gather is for the purpose of mission. They gather together to be refueled, recalibrated and prepped for the missions that are about to take place next—when the missionaries are sent into the places of their daily living.

MORE THAN LABELS

During the last few years the missional concept has gained traction and so has the idea of missional communities. But some churches have merely relabeled their small groups as missional communities. This reminds us of the 1980s project by General Motors. The car company took its four-cylinder Chevrolet Cavalier, fancied up the interior a bit, stuck Cadillac emblems on it and called it the Cadillac Cimarron. It was a disaster that's now referred to as "the car that nearly doomed Cadillac." Not only did the Cimarron fail to deliver on the respected Cadillac name, it cheapened the brand and crippled it for several years thereafter.

The approach taken by many small group leaders is to organize projects and outreach tasks for members to participate in. That is all well and good. We should join together for particular outreaches from time to time. But that doesn't make a small group a missional community. What is really needed on a regular basis is for everyday Christians to be on everyday mission. It is a mistake to think of missional communities as groups that do mission together. We prefer to think of them as groups of missionaries.

Other group leaders have made more thoughtful efforts to help their groups become genuinely missional entities. One of the most important steps in this reengineering process is to give the communities their proper place of importance in our overall church mission. We found the following quote from Charles Olsen in a book he wrote four decades ago to be poignant for today:

> Although small groups have been utilized as a church renewal scheme, they have rarely been legitimized as a full expression of the church. They have been conceived as an adjunct for the personal growth of the participants. They have been considered an "extra" in church programming,

and they have served this role well. Meanwhile the "real" church gathers in the sanctuary at eleven each Sunday. It's there, with "everybody" (except the sick, etc.) present, that the sacraments of baptism and the Lord's Supper are celebrated. We have been so oriented toward the gathered congregation that the small group is relegated to serving as a means to a larger end—that is, to stimulate active participation in the corporate congregation.[3]

When we look at small groups as secondary helper units for bolstering our larger gatherings we have gone off the rails. The better view is to see our corporate gatherings—church services—as a celebratory exclamation point of lives lived as salt and light the previous week.

KOINONIA—MORE THAN "KUMBAYA" AND COOKIES

The word *fellowship* has become a synthetic filler for just about all things church-related. We make announcements that say, "Join together next Sunday for the big game, where we will have fun, food and fellowship." Or we talk about the good feeling we had as "a great time of fellowship." The Greek word *koinonia* is phenomenally richer than such surfacey concepts of fellowship. Just as church is not an event or location, neither is fellowship. The best translation for the word *fellowship* is "partnership." Justo Gonzalez shines light on the beauty of biblical *koinonia*:

> In Philippians 3:10, what the Revised Standard Version translates as "share his sufferings" actually says "know the *koinonia* of his sufferings." In 1 Corinthians 10:16, Paul says, "The cup of blessing which we bless, is it not a participation in the blood of Christ?" The term that the Revised Standard Version translates here as "participation," with a footnote explaining that it could also be translated

as "communion," is *koinonia.* Paul's letter to the Philippians, which acknowledges receipt of a gift, begins with words in which Paul is thanking the Philippians for their partnership and sharing with him. In 1:5, he says that he is thankful for the Philippians' *koinonia,* and two verses later he declares that they are "joint *koinonoi*" of grace with him, that is, common owners or sharers. At the end of the epistle, he says that they have shared in his trouble (4:14), and the term he uses could be translated as "cokoinonized." All of this leads to the unique partnership "in giving and receiving" that he has enjoyed with the church of the Philippians (4:15), and once again the word he uses literally means "koinonized." In short, *koinonia* is much more than a feeling of fellowship; it involves sharing goods as well as feelings.[4]

Notice the tangibility of true fellowship as described by Gonzalez. The only thing at stake when we show up with a bowlful of Chex Mix at most small groups is that we may not have any leftovers to take home. But when I bring my calendar, checkbook and confessions to the group, the stakes shoot high and I have relational skin in the game.

Most Christians have never experienced genuine biblical fellowship. Therefore most of us have missed out on the very essence and flavor of the good news of the kingdom of God. What should be one of the most compelling aspects of our witness to a watching world is lost in the face of the watered-down version of fellowship we have settled for. Scholar Norman Kraus speaks to the missional attractiveness of the faithful community of believers:

> In the New Testament, repentance means renouncing our old self-centered life and adopting the new lifestyle of agape (love) demonstrated by Jesus. This same community,

which exists "by grace through faith," is also the community of witness. . . . It has the character of a movement always remaining in and for the world. Jesus described it as a "city set on a hill," whose light beckons and guides the weary, lost traveler to the security and camaraderie of a civilized society. In the city there was safety from the marauders who took advantage of the darkness to rob and kill. In a friendly city foreigners could find protection and hospitality. Thus Jesus used the city as a symbol of the saving community, whose light shines in the gathering darkness, inviting the traveler to find salvation.[5]

The early Christian communities threw themselves into one-anotherness. They didn't bring Jesus into their individual lives. They entered into a family. Their old life was dead and their new life was in Christ and lived out among a new family. Jesus and the writers of the Epistles use familial language across the pages of the New Testament. On one occasion Jesus was told that his mother and brothers were outside of the house where he was staying and were requesting to see him. He answered, "'Who is my mother, and who are my brothers?' Pointing to his disciples, he said, 'Here are my mother and my brothers'" (Mt 12:48-49). To enter into early-days Christianity meant you were part of "the Way" (Acts 19:9, 23; 24:14, 22). You set aside your individualism and became a member.

In their letters to the churches the apostles don't let us skate by on hollow definitions of love. They hold our feet to the fire that is the cost of loving one another by demanding substance and action, not mere words. Missing from modern translations is the phrase "unfeigned love," used by both Paul and Peter (2 Cor 6:6; 1 Pet 1:22 KJV). This is a great old-school phrase that means sincere—not faked. The apostles are saying, in essence,

"Don't give us words of love without deeds." Peter tells us to practice "unfeigned love of the brethren." Missional communities are those of us who take seriously these admonitions by crafting lifestyles that respond to the word of Jesus and the gospel of the kingdom of God. Eugene Peterson echoes this in his paraphrase of James 2:

> Dear friends, do you think you'll get anywhere in this if you learn all the right words but never do anything? Does merely talking about faith indicate that a person really has it? For instance, you come upon an old friend dressed in rags and half-starved and say, "Good morning, friend! Be clothed in Christ! Be filled with the Holy Spirit!" and walk off without providing so much as a coat or a cup of soup— where does that get you? Isn't it obvious that God-talk without God-acts is outrageous nonsense? (Jas 2:14-17 *The Message*)

The cost of living a biblical Christianity strikes at middle-class sensibilities focused on the American Dream. In my book with Alan Hirsch, *Right Here, Right Now*, Hirsch writes,

> Genuine biblical faith in God takes us to a place that is beyond intellectual ascent and a mere collation of correct ideas about God. It transforms us into carriers and transmitters of the very love that rescued us in the first place. There is a clear and distinct connection between God and the lifestyles that should be produced from a living encounter with God. Middle-class culture is all too often contrary to the values of the gospel: the gospel brand of love directly challenges our consumeristic obsession with comfort and convenience and our middle-class preoccupation with safety and security.[6]

One can only imagine the impact that a style of Christianity lived out in the family of faith could make on the culture. What would Christianity look like if we responded to one another the same way we do to our natural family members when we become aware of their needs?

MUTUAL-ACCOUNTABILITY CULTURES

We must never lose sight of the fact that we are not individually the body of Christ. It is the collective diversity of wisdom, skill, experience and spiritual gifting that manifests the *corpus Christi*. But the individualistic mindset of Western Christianity clouds this view. Along with this, we often struggle with a leadership-centric mentality that views accountability as upward-focused, scaling the vertical ladder of hierarchy. The New Testament demonstrates, models and teaches something very different—mutual accountability. Len Hjalmarson writes, "When we no longer see dominance and social influence as the basic activities of leadership, we no longer think of people in terms of leaders and followers. Instead, we can think of leadership as a process in which an entire community is engaged."[7]

Granted, it is extremely difficult for us to reorient our minds around the upside-down ways of Jesus and his kingdom. Leadership as practiced in the world's system—what Jesus called the ways of the Gentiles—is what constitutes our concept of accountability. Christians don't think in terms of mutual accountability, and most pastors and church leaders don't teach this mode either. The subject of church discipline, for instance, is usually taught as the job of elders and top-dog church leaders. But this concept is unfounded when a thorough study of the New Testament is undertaken.

One of the first questions I am asked when I enter into a conversation or teach from the concepts in my book *UnLeader* hinges on the issue of accountability. "But who do people answer to?" is what people usually ask. The answer is, "We are accountable to one another." Again, the ethos emerging from four decades of church growth focus is that the church is a business or corporation, with vertical charts of hierarchy. Contrary to that, the language of the New Testament is that of church as family, as we discussed earlier.

Paul declares his belief that the body of Christ is competent and equipped to sufficiently carry out the task of admonishing one another. Recall that the epistle to the Romans is not addressed to a senior committee, lead pastor or even the elders of the church. Instead Paul writes to the collective that is the believing community: "Now I myself am confident concerning you, my brethren, that you also are full of goodness, filled with all knowledge, able also to admonish one another" (Rom 15:14 NKJV).

Paul has full confidence in the goodness, knowledge and ability of the body of Christ—everyday believers. He places the responsibility of warning and exhorting one another squarely on the shoulders of the collective community of believers. The first line of responsibility for social order and group harmony resides with the community as a whole. Page after page of the Epistles, verse after verse, emphasizes the responsibility of the family of God to rebuke when necessary and edify at all times. Here is a sampling of such passages:

- Honor one another (Rom 12:10).

- Build one another up (Rom 14:19; 1 Thess 5:11; Heb 3:13; 10:25).

- Warn and exhort one another (Rom 15:14; Col 3:16).

- Provide discipline among yourselves (1 Cor 5:3-5).

- Bear one another's overwhelming burdens (Gal 5:13; 6:2).

- Submit to one another (Eph 5:21).

- Teach one another (Col 3:16).

- Incite one another to love and good works (Heb 10:24).

- Confess sins to one another (Jas 5:16).

Church discipline is not to be carried out by a hierarchical few. It is the responsibility of the everyday saints to carry it out.[8] In her book *Followership* Barbara Kellerman provides insight into the underappreciated influence of sibling relationships:

> The new science of siblings confirms that the impact on us of our equals (siblings) rivals that of our superiors (parents) even as early as childhood. By the time children are eleven years old, they spend approximately 33 percent of their free time with their siblings, more than they spend with their parents, teachers, friends, or even by themselves. In fact, from the time they are born, our brothers and sisters are our collaborators and co-conspirators, our role models and cautionary tales. What we can say, then, is that followers follow each other first and foremost because they model their behavior on others similar to themselves. Followers also follow other followers for some of the same reasons they follow their leaders. That is, followers go along with other followers because they (1) lend stability and security, (2) provide order and meaning, and (3) constitute the group to which they want to belong. Of course, when followers follow other followers, as opposed to following their leaders, formal rank plays little or even no meaningful role. No one is designated superior—which means no one is the designated subordinate. We see this in informal groups, such as children together in a playground.[9]

Our obsession with the concept of a single, buck-stops-here leader has obscured the New Testament theme of the family of God as the most frequently used metaphor for the interactive relationship of the church. We need to relearn these attitudes and practices in the context of missional community groups. This is not to say that people do not have responsibilities they must answer for. But nowhere do we find the idea of a boss-employee arrangement in the New Testament. What we see is a commitment to self-discipline, accountability to the group as a whole, and personal responsibility.

Learning to live in the depths of biblical *koinonia* requires an altogether new set of skills, commitment to selflessness and submission of ourselves into the hands of a broad community. Biblically functioning missional communities live from interdependent foci. The habits, skills and practices of interdependence at the level we find in the New Testament are not mere add-ons or slight adjustments to the way we carry out our lives. This type of living necessitates cataclysmic change to the way we do life. That is the way it always is in the kingdom of God.[10]

Agreeing to certain dance steps brings a rhythm to the life of our communities. But it is not rigid. It allows for nuance, and no two dances are ever exactly the same even though they follow the same steps. When we commit to a common set of missional habits regarding mutual accountability and encouragement, a certain synergy develops. Each member starts to live out the apostolic commandment to "stir up one another to love and good works" (Heb 10:24 ESV).

In the most famous sermon ever preached, the Sermon on the Mount, Jesus told his followers, "You are the light of the world. A town built on a hill cannot be hidden. Neither do people light a lamp and put it under a bowl. Instead they put it on its stand, and it gives light to everyone in the house. In the same way, let your light shine before others, that they may see your good deeds and glorify your Father in heaven." (Mt 5:14-16).

In the group guide Brad and I wrote called *Missional Essentials*, we drew our cue from this familiar passage and developed a set of practices based on the word *light* as a set of habits for missional communities. Let's look at them:

L: *Listen to the Holy Spirit.* Commit to at least one hour per week of listening to the promptings of the Holy Spirit. Some members may choose to take a prayer walk or carve out a once-per-week time of solitude and listening to God. Others may segment their hour into daily increments of say ten minutes per day for six days of the week. The point is to have a specific time of just listening in silence, not speaking or asking for anything, just letting the Lord speak to you.

I: *Invite others to share a meal.* Share at least three meals each week with others. Think in terms of people who are part of your faith community and of those who, as far as you know, are not Christ-followers. Share a meal with someone from each category. The third meal can be with someone from either category. The idea is that around the table, gospel things happen.

G: *Give a blessing.* Seek to do three acts of blessing a week: one to a member of the Christian community, one to a non-Christian and one from either category, as with the sharing of meals. Blessings can range from a simple email of encouragement to a gift of some sort. You are purposely seeking to be a blessing to your faith community and the broader world as well.

H: Hear from the Gospels. Commit to read from the Gospels each week in order to specifically learn more about Jesus, his ways and means. The Gospels are always included in the weekly rhythm so that we constantly stay Jesus-centered. It is vital to read from other books of the Bible as part of your spiritual formation, but always include Gospel reading as part of your regular habit.

T: Take inventory of the day. This is a consistent reminder that we are God's sent people. As a faith community, we are a missional collective. We want to stay mindful of opportunities to engage in mission on our day-to-day journey. To do this keep a daily journal of how you have worked with Jesus during the day. Ask yourself how you responded to his promptings and if there were any instances or opportunities where you resisted Jesus during the day.[11]

As missional communities meet together—weekly, twice per month or monthly—the LIGHT habits serve another purpose. Members have been living by them in their day-to-day lives, and now LIGHT becomes the outline for the sharing portion of the group time. Our suggestion is for groups to break into micro-groups of three to four people and to go through each of the five letters, sharing personal observations, experiences and learnings from the previous week.

One person may share her experience of meditating on a Gospel passage and responding to it later in the week while at the grocery store. The practice of prayerfully listening to the voice of the Holy Spirit has sharpened her ears and heightened her attentiveness to cues from God and she tells the story of responding by paying for a stranger's groceries. These are the ways the LIGHT habits frequently play out. Each habit tends to inform the others, creating a natural lifestyle that becomes a supernatural *light*-style.

STEPS ON THE QUEST

Try using LIGHT as a small group practice for a set time. Consider trying it out with a church staff or leadership team first, practicing the LIGHT habits for a month or two to develop a rhythm. After this trial run, invite five people to share their experience. Consider implementing LIGHT into the regular practice of your church's group life.

The writer of Hebrews encourages believing communities to consider "how to stir up one another to love and good works" (Heb 10:24 ESV). Surely you remember as a child (many of us still do this) mixing chocolate syrup into a glass of milk and stirring it up to get the milk and the chocolate combined. The more you put into the stirring, the chocolatier the milk becomes. Missional communities do the same thing. They actively engage in thoughtful practices that bring out the best in one another— stirring each other up to get the potential goodness and love spread all around.

8

Follow the Follower

Developing a Missional Leadership Approach

Lance Ford

• • •

*Unless the LORD builds the house,
the builders labor in vain.*

PSALM 127:1

I will build my church.

JESUS

Most *Jesus-followers* have fantasized about being one of the original Twelve. Our minds are captivated by the thought of what it must have been like to spend more than three years walking around, eating together, praying together and joking around with Jesus—in the flesh. We like to think we would be different from those guys. Surely we would get what Jesus meant in the parables. We wouldn't lack faith on so many occasions and would not ask so many dumb questions. And certainly we would understand Jesus when he spelled out his concepts of his kingdom. Wouldn't we?

As with any lengthy text, some of the most telling words of Scripture appear at first to be rather mundane statements. We have read many such verses hundreds if not thousands of times without actually hearing what the writer is saying. Toward the end of the Gospel of Matthew we come across one of these velvet brick statements that does not seem to offer any particularly stunning revelation: "Jesus left the temple and was walking away when his disciples came up to him to call his attention to its buildings" (Mt 24:1).

Our tendency is to jump past that first verse in order to get to the gist of the passage. It seems clear enough: Jesus left when the church service was over. But there is more meat on the bone of this verse. At this point in the Gospel narrative we are approaching the end and the disciples still don't get it. Jesus has spent more than three years pouring his life and thoughts into these guys, but they are still stuck in the familiar. The tires of their intellect are spinning in the muck of systemic hypnosis. Their minds remain wrapped around what they have always known. Let's read it again. Matthew says, "Jesus left the temple and was walking away . . . "

Forget Elvis leaving the building. Here we see that Jesus has left it. In this verse we see him walking away from the temple structure. Make no mistake: Matthew is pointing to something much more significant than it might first appear. Seismic changes are taking place. Throughout the Gospel of Matthew Jesus has frequented the temple, but this is the last time we see him there. For the rest of the book we do not see Jesus enter the temple. And in Matthew 24:1 he is not just walking away from the temple building. He is walking away from the entire temple system.

This is beyond the scope of anything the disciples can conjure. Their imaginations are shackled, held captive to the system they have known their entire lives. Plus they have their sights set on being in charge. Surely the day is drawing near when Jesus will be head rabbi and they'll be running the show for him. The disciples don't want Jesus to walk away from the temple and they are determined to draw his attention back. They're still hoping for some way to keep the system intact. To keep it going. Surely there are at least parts that are redeemable. Hasn't Jesus heard of throwing the baby out with the bath water? No such luck. Jesus finally spells it out by saying that every stone of the temple will lose cohesion and be brought down (Mt 24:2). In today's vernacular, Jesus says, "It's going down, baby!"

Decades later a seasoned apostle Peter reflects on those wonderful times of training alongside Jesus. As a young disciple full of great ideas and renegade spice he suffered public rebukes from Jesus directly and from Paul as well. But now he gets it. Peter has developed a deep understanding of what Jesus was about all along. It's plausible that Peter was thinking about that day, the moment when he and the other disciples stood in the street and tried to get Jesus refocused on the temple, when he wrote the letter to the Christians living in the Mediterranean basin:

> As you come to him, the living Stone—rejected by humans but chosen by God and precious to him—you also, like living stones, are being built into a spiritual house to be a holy priesthood, offering spiritual sacrifices acceptable to God through Jesus Christ. (1 Pet 2:4-5)

Systems can be addictive and captivating. They become what we are familiar with—our comfort zone. Peter's imagination is no longer hostage to the old system and he wants to make it clear for the church. He must convey to the saints that the Lord has a new temple and a new priesthood system for that temple. Jesus has fulfilled his own prophecy that three days after his crucifixion his physical body would be resurrected, and so it is with the mystical body of Christ—the church will also rise. Jesus-followers will rise up as a new temple, replacing the limiting hierarchical system of privileged priests. The plain people will become priests.

PLAYING WITH A FULL DECK

One barrier that cannot be ignored if we hope to fulfill the missional quest is the challenge of the professionalization of ministry—what is commonly referred to as the clergy-laity divide. Though the word *laity* literally means "the people," its popular meaning refers to a nonprofessional. We might speak of a person who uses plumbing each day—with little understanding of pipes—as a layperson. Contrast that to a plumber, who is an expert and a professional on the subject. "My grandmother was good with home remedies," someone might say, "but she was just a layperson. She was no doctor."

A layperson is thought to be a person who dabbles in a subject or skill but has no formal training or expertise. The trusted answers are to be found at the feet of the professionals. The tough jobs should be left to the professionals. In the church world, the word *clergy* connotes the idea of professional priest. Despite the fact that the New Testament gives no hint whatsoever of this concept, it is the paradigm and posture of most Christian churches. Of course, we need ministers whose vocational income comes through ministry. We have accounts of this in the New Testament. The problem is an overemphasis on professional ministry that has left most Christians not seeing themselves as part of the *missio Dei*. They relegate themselves to the spectators' stands because they fail to see their own value and giftedness to participate fully. It's like playing a football game with only two or three of your eleven allotted players on the field. It is a recipe for defeat.

To divide the body of Christ into a clergy-laity distinction incapacitates the church as a movement. It is a brilliant scheme on the part of Satan because it cuts the body off at the legs. For there to be any hope for a "normal" Christian to gain a personal vision of his or her calling to ministry, regardless of vocation, we must join Jesus and "leave the temple." By that we do not mean that we should all abandon church buildings and do house church. We are not out to eliminate organization, or even institutions in all forms. But we must disentangle ourselves from institutionalism and change the way we have organized ourselves and the household of God. We need to eliminate the idea of ministry as office and reclaim the biblical idea of ministry as function. Toward this goal, let's look at a familiar passage from the apostle Paul's letters:

> But to each one of us grace has been given as Christ apportioned it. This is why it says:
>
>> "When he ascended on high,
>>   he took many captives
>>   and gave gifts to his people."
>
> (What does "he ascended" mean except that he also descended to the lower, earthly regions? He who descended is the very one who ascended higher than all the heavens, in order to fill the whole universe.) So Christ himself gave the apostles, the prophets, the evangelists, the pastors and teachers, to equip his people for works of service, so that the body of Christ may be built up. (Eph 4:7-12)

Most churches and denominations view this passage under the lens of the clergy-laity divide. It is commonly understood as a leadership text. The mistake (and it's a huge one) is to read verses 11 and 12 as a standalone text. When we do so we interpret it as saying that Jesus provides five types of specialists (clergy or professional staff) to train the saints (laity or church members) to do ministry. Even with this interpretation, few church staffs actually set out to train church members to do full-on ministry. Church members are usually relegated to support roles that assist the staff, who are the ones actually doing the ministry. Tim Catchim and Alan Hirsch have this to say about the Ephesians 4 text:

> Paul says in verse 7, "But to each one of us [Greek *hekasto*] grace was given, according to the measure of Christ's gift." *Hekasto* literally means "to each and every person." He intends that we understand it quite literally to mean every person, that is, all believers hearing these words both then and now. Rather than gifts being given to an elite few and for the benefit of the many, these gifts are given to all and are for the benefit of all; it is the saints who equip the saints. Remember that the letter is written to, and intended to be read out in, the gathered ecclesia (the various house churches) in Ephesus and not to a leadership conference. It is addressed to all of the people of God as a whole, including women and slaves, and in all their nonprofessional glory. Furthermore, the hearers came from across the racial, social, economic, and gender spectrum. This means that every believer fits into the APEST (apostle, prophet, evangelist, shepherd, teacher) typology! This is a deeply radicalizing text that has huge ramifications for how we both recognize and unleash the ministry of every believer.[1]

> ### STEPS ON THE QUEST
>
> *Identify the APEST (apostle, prophet, evangelist, shepherd, teacher) people in your church or faith community. Is there a mixture of gender, clergy, laity and socioeconomic status? Which people in your church are "diamonds in the rough" regarding their APEST gifts? Could they be helped by mentoring?*

Historically the most significant movements in Jesus' name have been grassroots thrusts by plain old Jesus folk who tired of the established churches they were attached to—churches that had become nonmovemental. Most parachurch ministries from the latter twentieth century began as missional movements to reach people and meet needs that the static church was either ignoring or unable to reach because of their institutionalized systems and structures. Many of these ministries today reach across the globe, led well by the laity—the people—many of whom have never attended Bible college or seminary or held a position as a church staff member. The God-ignited fire in their hearts drives them out of the most commonly recognized church structures into the world as servants for the kingdom of God. And the static church world calls these ministries "parachurch"? We believe that is a derogatory term. Ministries such as Youth with a Mission, InterVarsity, Navigators and so on are through-and-through the faithful church—the gathered people of God—on mission.

John Wimber, the leader of the Vineyard movement that exploded across the globe throughout the 1980s, was fond of saying, "Everybody gets to play." He wanted every man, woman, boy and girl to know they were called to ministry and service.

The Gospels paint a picture of the low-rung commoners as Jesus' closest followers. It is the poor, the lame, the unclean, the outsiders, sinners and ex-communicated who pursue him and find entry into his fellowship. Contrast these people to the ones who ultimately crucify Jesus. It is the insiders, the power brokers such as the scribes, elders, chief priests and pawns of the Roman government who disparage Jesus and ultimately execute him.

As Richard Rohr has said, "Every point of view is a view from a point," and Western Christians—leaders in particular—have read the Gospels from the insider perspective of those who are on top. The outsider view—that of the people on the bottom— has not been the focus of the clergy class, which has ruled for nearly seventeen hundred years now. We must stop reading the New Testament from the perspective of a hierarchical and privileged priesthood class and get behind the genuine priesthood of all believers.

Called to Servanthood

Let's face it. Forty years of church growth focus has failed to render churches that are producing any degree of measurable change in our culture. Sure, our churches are getting larger, but study after study reveals a downward trend in overall church growth and attendance. There are a few megachurches that are exceptions, but it is past time for us to admit that the evolution of the Western megachurch is in large part due to a shifting of the saints—i.e., believers moving from one church to another.

For the last twenty years the topic of leadership has captivated the minds of pastors and denominational leaders to a near hypnotic degree. We are fascinated with leadership to the point that it has become a $50 billion industry. Books, websites, blogs and conferences deluge pastors and church staff members with the call—everything rises or falls on leadership. Our hypercultivation of leadership has left followership and servanthood to wilt like an unwatered plant.

An even more egregious mistake has to do with the source of our leadership concepts and definitions and how this has caused us to drift away from where Jesus steered us. In the book *Un-Leader*, I spoke to this syndrome:

> The largest church leadership conferences each year include talks from corporate-business world stars and world famous CEOs who make no claim to be followers of Christ. The bookshelves of most pastors and church leaders are filled with solid collections of *New York Times* bestselling books on leadership, authored by corporate business gurus and political figures. Furthermore, twice as many books on Christian leadership are available on Amazon. com as compared to titles on discipleship. Leadership making has not only trumped disciple making but also trampled it and left it in the dust. Regarding servantship, look for books on it and you are up the proverbial creek without a paddle. I have not found one Christian book on serving as a coveted position in and of itself. When they get close to it, authors in the Christian leadership field (in my research) cannot help themselves but to use the phrase "servant-leader." "Leader" seems to always get squeezed in. Mere "servantship" is not considered enough.[2]

Survey the New Testament and you will find scant attention given by Jesus and the writers of the Epistles to the topic of leadership. This is probably why there are so many Christian books on leadership—because we have to go beyond the Bible to find much on it. As of this writing, on Amazon.com there were fewer than five hundred Christian books on the subject of serving, yet we found more than eight thousand Christian books on leadership. Contrary to what we have been taught, it is clear that Jesus believed his kingdom would rise or fall not on leadership but on servanthood.

To follow Jesus means to follow his lead. It means to live our lives by following the way he lived his life. It's a counter-intuitive thought, but the Gospels clearly show that Jesus was a follower. That statement will come across to some readers as near-blasphemous. It's almost unconscionable for us to think of Jesus as a follower. But he was the quintessential follower of our heavenly Father. To see Jesus was to see the Father (Jn 14:9). He wasn't seeking to get his own way or even to get noticed. Jesus said as much:

> For I did not speak on my own, but the Father who sent me commanded me to say all that I have spoken. I know that his command leads to eternal life. So whatever I say is just what the Father has told me to say. (Jn 12:49-50)

Jesus resonated humility and servitude to the Father. He was the greatest follower humankind has ever witnessed. This means that for us to follow him means we follow Jesus into the ways and means of followership over and above leadership. No objective reading of the Gospels presents Jesus as focusing whatsoever on training his disciples to be great leaders. He modeled and messaged a pattern of followership and servant-hood. From all this came tremendous leadership on behalf of the twelve, but their identity was not as "leaders."

This is where we have missed it in our leadership-centric obsession. Jesus leads us not to become great leaders but to become great servants: "The greatest among you should be like the youngest, and the one who rules like the one who serves" (Lk 22:26). This does not mean that leadership is unimportant. But it means that leadership in the kingdom of God is vastly different from the types of leadership we see exercised in the world's system. Leadership in the kingdom of God is a product of great followership and servanthood. The focus is not on who is the biggest dog in the yard. That was the very stuff Jesus forbade and crushed (see Mt 20:25-27). His disciples are never called to get people to follow them. Following Jesus' lead, the disciples were to constantly point away from themselves and unto the Father. When John the Baptist's disciples became somewhat upset about his dwindling ministry in light of Jesus' growing fame, John set them straight:

> An argument developed between some of John's disciples and a certain Jew over the matter of ceremonial washing. They came to John and said to him, "Rabbi, that man who was with you on the other side of the Jordan—the one you testified about—look, he is baptizing, and everyone is going to him."
>
> To this John replied, "A person can receive only what is given them from heaven. You yourselves can testify that I said, 'I am not the Messiah but am sent ahead of him.' The bride belongs to the bridegroom. The friend who attends the bridegroom waits and listens for him, and is full of joy when he hears the bridegroom's voice. That joy is mine, and it is now complete. He must become greater; I must become less." (Jn 3:25-30)

OUT OF FOCUS

More than two decades of hearing the mantra "Everything rises or falls on leadership" has diverted our eyes from the call of Jesus: "Make disciples." The leadership wake has created a generation of church leaders who are savvy at running churches but have scant skills and experience in the actual making of disciples. We view a recent article as telling in this regard. A joint research project conducted by the Exponential Church Planting Network and LifeWay Christian Resources was based on interviews with more than thirty well-known leaders who had more than six hundred years of cumulative experience working with hundreds of church planters. Ed Stetzer unpacks the findings on his blog:

> Leadership development is the most frequently cited challenge of planters according to our research in this survey of church planting leaders and thinkers. Leadership issues included recruiting and developing leaders, implementing teams, creating a reproducible leadership development approach, developing a leader/oversight/elder board, hiring and leading staff, discerning changes required to facilitate growth, healthy decision making, and delegating and empowering volunteers.[3]

In a subsequent blog post, Stetzer continues:

> I asked [Darrin Patrick], "Why do most churches stay small?" Darrin explained: Largely because most pastors don't know how to build systems, structures, and processes that are not contingent upon them. Most pastors can care for people, but don't build systems of care. Most pastors can develop leaders individually, but lack the skill to implement a process of leadership development. When a pastor can't build systems and structures that support ministry, the only people who are cared for or empowered to lead are those who are "near" the pastor or those very close to the pastor. This limits the size of the church to the size of the pastor.[4]

Todd Wilson, who leads the Exponential network, weighed in on the report:

> Discipleship is cited as a uniquely . . . separate thing from leadership development in the report. Where lead-

ership development is in the context of building the institution bigger, discipleship is in the context of growing
the believer better. . . . What if our paradigm of seeing
them as distinct . . . is actually part of the problem? Isn't
it strange that we are coming off two to three decades of
leadership . . . as the silver bullet (or pill) for everything
and now . . . we've entered a period where the most
elusive, frustrating issue for most pastors is with inef-
fectiveness in discipleship? Down deep most know . . .
we are struggling to make disciples who are a distinctly
different aroma to the world.[5]

We believe Wilson reaches the right conclusion. Our obsession with leadership—building the church—has choked out
the call to make disciples. We have had the wrong focus. The
irony here is that Jesus said he would take care of building his
church (see Mt 16:18), and while he does that he wants us to
make disciples (see Mt 28:19). It's as if we've told Jesus we want
his job. All the while we've left the job he gave us undone.

Leadership-centric cultures too often have little to no relational intelligence. There is too much distance between upper-
echelon church leaders and others such as lower-ranking staff
members, which is where discipleship should be taking place as
well. When this is the case it betrays the reality that there is no
authentic discipling relationship in play. Nannerl Keohane,
former president of Duke University, writes,

When we speak of "relationships," we usually have in
mind close, affectionate, enduring affiliations with a
parent, lover, husband, sibling, colleague, or friend. The
distinctive connection between leaders and followers is
not well captured by this term. In large organizations
leaders have many followers; followers have only one

leader (or a small number of leaders). The followers may feel that they "know" the leader through observing her in action, shaking her hand at a large gathering, receiving a certificate of commendation, or reading about the leader's family. On this basis, if they generally approve the leader's actions and sense any kind of personal warmth on the leader's part, they are indeed likely to feel that they do indeed have a direct, personal connection with the leader. But no leader can have a direct, personal connection with

Leadership-centric cultures too often have little to no relational intelligence.

large numbers of followers; this is possible only for those with whom he works most immediately. Occasional personal encounters with other followers can be meaningful to the leader, but they are rarely as important as they are for the follower. These "relationships" cannot, by their very nature, be symmetrical. So the connection between the leader and her followers must be more abstract, detached, and impersonal than the term "relationship" can usefully be expected to describe.[6]

THE "WITH ME" SYSTEM

Yet another verse that appears quite unassuming unveils Jesus' "strategic plan": "He appointed twelve that they might be *with him* and that he might send them out to preach" (Mk 3:14, emphasis added). What a simplistic plan. Jesus' disciple-making system was built around the idea of inviting a few people to join his life. His formula was not to invite people to a discipleship Bible study or a small group meeting, or even a men's accountability group. All of these can be wonderfully helpful resources along the disciple-making way, but none can substitute for what Jesus does.

They fail to do what the verse above calls for. Discipleship happens when one follower of Jesus invites another person to follow with her as she follows Jesus.

There is nothing like spending quality time with a person who is especially good at something. It's one thing to read books on woodworking and watch videos on the artistry and craftsmanship involved, but it's an altogether different and more enriching experience to spend time alongside a master craftsman. No amount of lectures or classroom time can produce the results of an actual in-the-field apprenticeship experience. Disciple making is no different. Pastors and ministry leaders must reimagine the concept.

Discipleship is a relational experience. It takes place as one Jesus-follower empowers another person by sharing his or her knowledge and experience of following Christ over a substantial period of time. The discipleship greenhouse is the environment of natural life rhythms. If you are an authentic discipler, you can point to a handful of folks you have opened up your life to. The question for all of us who claim faithfulness to the Great Commission is, "Who have I invited to be with me?" Furthermore, if we claim that our churches are faithful in discipleship, we must be able to point to a culture in our church that has this "be with me" ethos, not merely a "come to church with me" culture.

Younger converts need to hang out with seasoned Jesus veterans and watch how they live out the Christ life. At its core discipleship gives one follower the opportunity to see the Word of God enfleshed in the life of another human being. It is the practicing of the Word that makes the preaching of the Word come alive. Younger followers get the opportunity to say, "Oh, that's what it looks like when such-and-such verse is lived out." Robert Clinton and Paul Stanley convey the idea here:

Mentoring is as old as civilization itself. Through this natural relational process, experience and values pass from one generation to another. Mentoring took place among Old Testament prophets (Eli and Samuel, Elijah and Elisha) and leaders (Moses and Joshua), and New Testament leaders (Barnabas and Paul, Paul and Timothy). Throughout human history, mentoring was the primary means of passing on knowledge and skills in every field— from Greek philosophers to sailors—and in every culture. But in the modern age, the learning shifted. It now relies primarily on computers, classrooms, books, and videos. Thus, today the relational connection between the knowledge-and-experience giver and the receiver has weakened or is nonexistent.[7]

The content presented so far in this chapter is for the purpose of the missional quest. As we have said before, this is about a movement. We are all hoping to see the next great Jesus wave hit the world, and for that to happen it will come about through the folks—the everyday Christian living an everyday mission. If you are a pastor or are at the helm of a ministry in your church, it is incumbent on you to work with your team to cultivate an environment like we have described if you hope to see your church become a full-on missional church.

Early in my walk with Christ I intuitively knew I needed someone to guide me in the journey. I was attending the small church that my parents were part of, and having gotten to know the pastor somewhat I asked if he would mind meeting with me and helping me out. To be discipled was what I was asking for—I just didn't know what to call it. I still remember the look on his face when I approached him with the request. He was an extremely gifted preacher and could preach for an hour at a time, keeping everyone engaged with no problem. But when I asked him if we could spend time together he was at a loss for words. The color left his face and he stammered, "Uh—yeah . . . I guess so."

This man was a bivocational pastor who had a shop behind his house where he created dental appliances. I had envisioned just going and hanging out and talking as he went about his work. The first time I showed up at his house he invited me in and we sat in his living room with some prepublished study material that we read and discussed together for about forty-five minutes. After the "lesson" he walked me to the door and I headed home. We did this a couple more times and he told me I was "good to go," that me and the Holy Spirit would do just fine. The biggest smile I saw on his face during all our sessions was as he was waving to me as I drove off from the last meeting. I have little doubt that this pastor had never been involved in a discipling relationship. He most likely had never had anyone invite him on a "be with me" relationship, and he flat-out did not know what to do with it. But . . . he was a really good preacher.

Many leaders, if the truth were known, are just like my pastor. They have no idea of where to start with a discipling relationship. The idea can be even more daunting for "regular" church folk. Few church members envision themselves as being called to make disciples. We need to remove the mystique from disciple making. The reason the early church flourished and the Chinese church flourishes today is the simple discipleship ethos that Jesus modeled. Anyone who is a follower of Jesus is equipped to mentor others. The only requirement is a willingness to go on mission and share with others our lives and what we have learned from God.

Therefore go and make disciples of all nations, baptizing them in the name of the Father and of the Son and of the Holy Spirit, and teaching them to obey everything I have commanded you. (Mt 28:19-20)

MENTORING OTHERS

What has God taught you? What lessons have you learned along the way of following Jesus? What mistakes have you made and what decisions do you believe were right? The answers to these questions are yeast for missional disciple making. Followers of Jesus who are willing disciple makers pass along to others whatever God has given them that has enabled them to deepen their relationship with him. Younger believers need a "go-to" person in their life who will help them process and learn the art of spiritual response when facing difficult situations and relationships. Nothing can take the place of having someone say, "One time I found myself in a situation much like that and here's how I walked it out and here's the biblical reasoning I had in mind." In their book *Connecting*, Clinton and Stanley write,

> Our experience with mentoring and our focus on its use center on empowerment—the increased capacity of the mentoree generated by the mentoring relationship and the resources shared. In our survey of leaders, we found that almost all of them identified three to ten people who made significant contributions to their development. A study of major biblical figures and the biographies of Christian leaders clearly underscored the conclusion that one of the major influences most often used by God to develop a leader is a person or persons who have something to share that the leader needs. These

people who influenced others seemed to have some common characteristics.[8]

This list of notable characteristics shared by prolific mentors includes:

- Ability to readily see potential in a person.

- Willingness to tolerate mistakes, brashness, abrasiveness and the like in order to see that potential develop.

- Flexibility in responding to people and circumstances.

- Patience, knowing that time and experience are needed for development.

- Perspective, having vision and ability to see down the road and suggest the next steps a mentoree needs.

- Gifts and abilities that build up and encourage others.[9]

Think about the people who have made an impact on your life—maybe a grade school teacher, a high school coach, a Scout leader, an aunt or uncle—people who were not your parents or guardians. You can probably point to many if not all of the characteristics above when you think of how that person shaped your life. Mentors are willing to risk their own reputation for the sake of development of a mentoree. They are willing to give up their own playing time as well in order to give the disciple an opportunity to develop. Think of Jesus, sending out the twelve disciples in his own name to serve through preaching, healing and feeding others. His reputation was on the line on every occasion when they went out. Jesus was aware that some of his guys were going to mess things up from time to time. That is the price to pay if you want to see someone become a disciple.

STEPS ON THE QUEST

If you are a leader, ask yourself: Who am I currently mentoring? Have I invited anyone to be with me in a discipling relationship? Evaluate your church or faith community: Who are the everyday nonprofessionals that would be good at mentoring others in the fellowship? Be sure to think in terms of APEST (apostle, prophet, evangelist, shepherd, teacher). Are there younger believers—in either age or experience—who show certain gifts and who would benefit by being matched up with someone in a mentoring relationship that focuses on honing and maturing that particular gift?

9

Have a Great Trip

What Matters in the Long Run

• • •

They say Rome wasn't built in a day,
but I wasn't on that particular job.

BRIAN CLOUGH, ENGLISH FOOTBALL MANAGER

The true husbandman will cease from anxiety,
as the squirrels manifest no concern whether the woods will
bear chestnuts this year or not, and finish labor with every day,
relinquishing all claim to the produce of his fields,
and sacrificing in his mind not only his
first but his last fruits also.

HENRY DAVID THOREAU, WALDEN

On a soggy summer evening early in the final season of the 1950s, a thirty-three-year-old left-handed pitcher made major league baseball history. Pop! The sound of the ball hitting the catcher's mitt as the batter swung and missed signaled strike three, the final out of the ninth inning. Players swarmed to congratulate their teammate with back pats and "atta-boys". The pitcher had just retired twenty-seven consecutive batters. After nine innings the scoreboard read all zeroes. No runs, no hits, no errors, no walks. Though the powerhouse Milwaukee Braves team included sluggers such as Eddie Matthews and Hank Aaron, not one batter facing Pittsburgh Pirates pitcher Harvey Haddix had reached first base. It was the rarest of feats indeed.

Before that game there had been only six perfect games pitched in the history of the major leagues. But a caveat loomed. Harvey's Pirate teammates may have forgotten something in the midst of their excitement over his historic performance. The scoreboard had another zero. The game was not over. It was tied. Not one Pirates player had crossed home plate. Harvey would go on to pitch another amazing three innings, setting a record with each out. He ended up throwing twelve full innings of no-hit, perfect pitching. *Sports Illustrated* writer Albert Chen discusses the feat:

> "People ask me all the time what the most memorable game I've ever played in was," says Pirates second baseman Bill Mazeroski, who would hit his legendary World Series–winning home run against the New York Yankees a year later. "Half the time I tell them it was Game 7 of the '60 Series. The other half of the time I tell them it was the night Harvey Haddix threw the finest game in the history of baseball. Then they'll look at me and say, 'Harvey who?'"[1]

Why have so few people heard of Harvey Haddix and arguably the greatest game ever pitched? Because he lost the game. Harvey's team failed to score and the Braves ultimately reached the plate in the thirteenth inning. Final score: Braves 1, Pirates 0. To this day major league baseball refuses to recognize Harvey Haddix's accomplishment as a no-hitter, much less a perfect game. Haddix is listed in the official record books as the losing pitcher of that game.

No one wants to end up like Harvey Haddix and his Pittsburgh Pirate teammates. It is possible for church leaders to develop impressive statistics in relation to buildings, crowds, budgets and the like. All while they're losing the game when it comes to affecting their communities and cities and advancing the kingdom of God. As we've discussed, it's possible to grow a "great" church but fail to make disciples. It doesn't have to be this way—if church leaders will stop being enamored with just one side of the scoreboard.

Today we find ourselves in a similar situation to Harvey Haddix. We're putting up good numbers but still not winning the game. Every few months another report appears showing that though we have more megachurches than ever, Christianity is on decline overall in America. In a *USA Today* article labeling an emerging category of people who claim no religious affiliation as "Nones," Cathy Lynn Grossman writes,

> In the 1960s, two in three Americans called themselves Protestant. Now the Protestant group—both evangelical and mainline—has slid below the statistical waters, down to 48%, from 53% in 2007. Where did they go? Nowhere, actually. They didn't switch to a new religious brand, they just let go of any faith affiliation or label. This group, called "Nones," is now the nation's second-largest category only to Catholics, and outnumbers the top Protestant denomination, the Southern Baptists. The shift is a significant cultural, religious and even political change.[2]

Reports such as this are becoming alarmingly too common. We have become great at doing church—we're pitching great—but we must take a look at the other side of the scoreboard to make sure we're doing what it takes to win the game. It is not an overstatement to call the Christian situation a crisis. But don't lose hope.

Gloomy reports notwithstanding, all is not lost. Though many people are losing trust in institutional Christianity, they are not losing interest in spirituality—the things of God. This is even more reason for renewed expressions of the church. Genuine Jesus people are still appealing and always will be. We like to say, "Lead with Jesus and the church will follow." The first Jesus movement began on the streets and in the marketplace. People experienced life together, centered on the teachings of Jesus, and became collectives—folks living selflessly for the sake of one another and the hurting ones in the host community. The appeal of a salty and lit-up church will never go out of style or lose its appeal.

SIZE MATTERS

Most discussions of church metrics include the issue of counting people in terms of church attendance. We should not be too quick to criticize one another in this regard. Throughout the Gospels and the book of Acts group sizes were mentioned. We all know of the five thousand who were fed by Jesus, the one hundred twenty in the upper room and the three thousand souls added to the church (Acts 2:41). Desiring to grow is not bad in and of itself. And it is not bad to keep track of how many people attend your church services. The problem comes when we become fixated on these metrics, believing that we are winning the game because we post well in attendance categories.

Often we hear arguments that criticize the desire in leaders for church growth. And many people are convinced that missional church advocates are anti-church growth. We want to attest here that nothing could be further from our desire for the church. One of the signal voices from the missional movement, Charles Van Engen, writes,

The universal intention of God in the Old Testament, the gathering in the New Testament, the finding of the lost sheep, the building toward fullness, and the picture of growth all point to something in the Church's nature which makes it yearn to incorporate more and more people within itself. There are likewise many biblical images of the Church which suggest this earnest desire. Whether the church is viewed as the people of God, the new Israel, the sheepfold, the planting, the building, or the body, there is always a driving energy within it. This is the growth principle by which the Church has always expressed her nature in "yearning" to incorporate more and more men and women within the bounds of God's grace.[3]

The question all church leaders should keep before them is, "Why do I want my church to grow?"

In the months leading up to a Kansas City conference we co-founded, an email arrived in our inbox. The sender stated that he would never attend our conference until it was hosted in a different venue—the fact that we were holding it in a large church proved that we were not "serious about the missional movement." What this person had not bothered to do was investigate the history of the host church. This church hosts about fifty different group events at its campus each month—none of which are church-related. The church in question has become a virtual community center for the surrounding neighborhood. Its mantra is that the building is a tool for the kingdom of God and a gift to the community.

If you are a pastor or a leader in a large church you need not apologize for having a large church or a large building. The issue is what you are doing with those resources and people power. Our aim as leaders should be transformation in the lives of the people the Lord has sent us to. The most important metrics therefore are in relation to life change and how our changed members are changing the host culture. The danger of focusing on the in-house side of the scoreboard is that we can fail to realize we're not scoring—our church, the people themselves, are not influencing their stations in life. If this is the case then we may have a wonderful saltbox, but the salt is staying in the box and not getting into the shakers. Reflecting on his pastorate, Alan Hirsch writes,

> One of the reflections arising out of my fifteen years' experience at [my church] is that as we grew and began to operate in the classic church growth mode it became increasingly harder to find God in the midst of the progressively more machinelike apparatus required to "run a church." With numerical growth, it seemed that we were increasingly being drawn away from the natural rhythms of life, from direct ministry, and that our roles seemed to become more managerial than ever before. But this mechanization of ministry was not only felt by the leadership of the church; the people in the church were increasingly being programmed out of life and therefore less engaged in active relationships with those outside of the faith community.[4]

THE LONG RUN

In the early 1980s Dick Vermeil, head coach of the Philadelphia Eagles, became the face of the term *burnout* when he retired from coaching at the age of 46—young for a head coach. Tales of Vermeil's drivenness to win a championship to the point of obsession became legendary. Night after night he slept on his office couch and never took a day off, which led to his flaming out in just a few years of coaching. Vermeil did this in the shadow of multiple–Super Bowl–winning coaches Don Shula,

Tom Landry and Chuck Knoll, who were in the midst of carving out careers that would each last more than two decades. He outworked all three of these Hall of Fame coaches but didn't come close to outwinning them.

Vermeil stayed out of the game until returning in his sixties to coach the downtrodden St. Louis Rams. Much older and with less stamina than his younger self, he had learned from the mistakes of his stress-filled, workaholic, worryaholic days in Philadelphia. Vermeil parlayed the patience he had acquired in his "retirement" years into a comeback yielding a Super Bowl championship with the Rams. He had learned that working smarter was better than working harder.

The missional quest takes patience. The best advice we give leaders who are trying to find their way down the missional path is "Take it easy." Work hard, but work even smarter. And above all things, leave the results to the Lord. He is the Lord of the harvest. Work the field, tend the crops, but at the end of the day grab your favorite drink, kick back and enjoy. Don't take yourself too seriously. You are yoked to a big, powerful ox. Let Jesus grow and build his church. Hear his words:

> Then Jesus said, "God's kingdom is like seed thrown on a field by a man who then goes to bed and forgets about it. The seed sprouts and grows—he has no idea how it happens. The earth does it all without his help: first a green stem of grass, then a bud, then the ripened grain. When the grain is fully formed, he reaps—harvest time! (Mk 4:26-29 *The Message*)

If you are a pastor or a leader in a church just setting out on the missional quest, you must be patient. Two thousand years of Christendom will not be extracted from your church in short order. Many church leaders have the makeup of entrepreneurs.

They see a problem and move quickly to fix it. But to move an existing church with a "come to us" approach as its primary expression toward a missional-incarnational approach is going to take tons of patience. Even if your church is young, most likely many or most of your members have a history of Christendom within their psyche. Give them time to process the missional theology and practices—including changes—it necessitates.

Think about this. How long have you been studying a missional approach? How many books have you read on the subject? How much time have you spent at conferences, conversing with peers, reading Internet blogs and articles? Have you searched the Scriptures on the subject? If so, you have been processing the concept for quite some time. You may be a wonderful communicator and a gifted preacher, but it's unreasonable and unfair to expect your church to jump on the missional train just because you preach a four-week series on the subject. Don't try to harvest fruit that is still in seedling form.

There will certainly be early adopters, but almost ninety percent of your congregation most likely will not be. The good news is that you need only about sixteen percent to begin what Malcolm Gladwell calls the "tipping point":

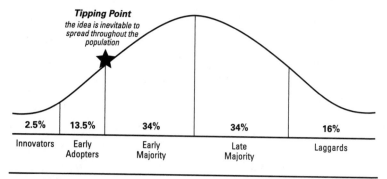

Figure 9.1. The tipping point

In Everett Rogers's 1962 book *Diffusion of Innovations*, Rogers defines an innovation as "an idea, practice, or object that is perceived as new by an individual or other unit of adoption."[5] The theory is that innovations flow along sectors of social systems that give rise or fall to new concepts or ideas. Potential buy-in moves along predictable pathways. The innovators and early adopters are the two vital people groups linked to the tipping point of a new idea seeking to gain traction within a social system. If these groups buy in to the idea it is inevitable, the new idea or concept will take off throughout the population. The job of leaders is to know who these people are in our midst. They play key roles for successful change and innovation.

In their book *On the Verge*, Alan Hirsch and Dave Ferguson speak of the importance of innovators and early adopters in relation to transitioning a church or faith community toward a missional ethos:

> In every group there are innovators: those who ignite the change before all others. The 2.5 percent of us who are innovators spark change in the 13.5 percent of those who are early adopters, and when you reach 16 percent of the group, the mission burns so red-hot, everyone can feel it.[6]

Speaking of the process of change toward missional imagination that took place in his own church, Community Christian Church in Naperville, Illinois, Ferguson writes:

> Our first efforts to spark the missional imagination of the people at Community came when we identified the innovators—the people who were already doing it and/or trying to do it. This small group of people came together several times to share what efforts they were already plotting on their own and to learn from one another. From this group

came some successes and also a lot of failures. We learned some things about what didn't work and what does work, and we put together a library of stories that would ignite the imagination of any Christ follower toward mission. It is by experimentation and pilot projects that you first enroll the 2.5 percent, who in turn influence the 13.5 percent and, over time, the whole church.[7]

KNOWING THE SCORE

We believe that every church should have some form of self-diagnostics to know its progress as a movement of the kingdom of God. In missional churches the effectiveness of the leaders is measured not by what they do or do not accomplish but by how the people of God are equipped, enabled, organized and inspired to participate in God's mission in the world.[8] We need to honestly evaluate our status in regard to our stated mission and purpose of existing as a local fellowship. We offer the following set of questions for churches to use in measuring progress toward the missional ethos:

1. *What are we here for?* You can't ask, "How's business?" if you are not clear on the "What business?" question. Missional churches clearly state their purpose for existence as it relates to the missional mandate laid out by Jesus and how that mandate informs their particular context. Mission is the organizing principle and the axis of the church. How would you describe your church's unique context and calling? Every church or missional community should use the answer to this question as a compass to recalibrate back to as it journeys on the missional quest.

2. *What are we currently doing?* Whatever a person or organization is doing with its time and resources is leading it somewhere. The things a church is doing are indicators of where it's

heading. Leaders need to ask the hard questions pertaining to their churches' faithfulness to their stated callings—i.e., how does question 2 line up with question 1?

3. *What should we stop doing? What should we start doing?* Be ruthless with these questions but don't be narrow-minded. The purists among us will seek to cut away everything they perceive as fat in a dramatic and abrupt fashion. Remember that we are a family. The Lord has called us to get a job done, but he also calls us to enjoy the journey. The journey is a long one and even slight coordinate changes will help us get on course. Prayerfully consider and make the course corrections needed to move toward your missional goals, but don't make sudden jerks of the rudder that cause people to be flung overboard.

4. *How will we know we are on course?* This question causes us to develop markers or signposts that help us know where we are on our journey. How many people are in discipling relationships? What percentage of our members know their neighbors and what percentage of our members' neighbors have shared meals in their homes? What are the "kingdom come on (our) earth" issues in your city or the immediate community around your church's epicenter? These indicators need to be very specific to your ministry context.

Missional metrics must be "out of the house" measurements—in other words, what's happening beyond our church services? Otherwise they're not missional metrics but church metrics. Perhaps the best way to assess the progress of a faith community in regard to missionality is its stories. How many stories are there and what is being championed in them? We covered the subject of storytelling in detail in chapter three but we feel we must conclude by reemphasizing the importance of stories.

If you are not hearing missional stories from the everyday members of your church, this is a needle marker of where your church is on the missional quest. On the flip side, if you are hearing stories from "the folks," then the water is rising on missionality within your fellowship. The people who tell these stories are the innovators in your midst. Keep in mind that just because you're not hearing stories does not mean they're not out there. Leaders need to be sure they are listening for stories. Make sure there's a way for the stories to be heard—a way for your church to collect and tell stories. It's possible that some wonderful missional activity is happening right under your noses but you're unaware.

The missional quest can and should be a wonderful journey. This doesn't mean it's an easy trek. Missional questers face demands of sacrifice, risk, faith and patience. Remember, Aslan is not safe. But he is good. Christians have been great at absorbing knowledge but have had a lesser propensity toward practice. Our hope is that you put what we have shared in this text to the test of your own life and the corporate life of those you have been called to journey alongside.

Appendix

"Sending Passages" in John's Gospel

SENDING AND THE FATHER

For God did not send his Son into the world to condemn the world, but to save the world through him. (Jn 3:17)

For the one whom God has sent speaks the words of God. (Jn 3:34)

Whoever does not honor the Son does not honor the Father, who sent him. (Jn 5:23)

Very truly I tell you, whoever hears my word and believes him who sent me has eternal life. (Jn 5:24)

I seek not to please myself but him who sent me. (Jn 5:30)

The works that the Father has given me to finish—the very works that I am doing—testify that the Father has sent me. And the Father who sent me has himself testified concerning me. (Jn 5:36-37)

For I have come down from heaven not to do my will but to do the will of him who sent me. (Jn 6:38)

No one can come to me unless the Father who sent me draws them. (Jn 6:44)

I am not here on my own authority, but he who sent me is true. You do not know him, but I know him because I am from him and he sent me. (Jn 7:28-29)

I am with you for only a short time, and then I am going to the one who sent me. (Jn 7:33)

I am one who testifies for myself; my other witness is the Father, who sent me. (Jn 8:18)

He who sent me is trustworthy. (Jn 8:26)

The one who sent me is with me. (Jn 8:29)

I have come here from God. I have not come on my own; God sent me. (Jn 8:42)

As long as it is day, we must do the works of him who sent me. (Jn 9:4)

Whoever believes in me does not believe in me only, but in the one who sent me. The one who looks at me is seeing the one who sent me. (Jn 12:44-45)

The Father who sent me commanded me to say all that I have spoken. (Jn 12:49)

Whoever accepts me accepts the one who sent me. (Jn 13:20)

These words you hear are not my own; they belong to the Father who sent me. (Jn 14:24)

They know you, the only true God, and Jesus Christ, whom you have sent. (Jn 17:3)

As you sent me into the world, I have sent them into the world. (Jn 17:18)

They know that you have sent me. (Jn 17:25)

Sending and the Son

Very truly I tell you, whoever accepts anyone I send accepts me. (Jn 13:20)

As you sent me into the world, I have sent them into the world. (Jn 17:18)

As the Father has sent me, I am sending you. (Jn 20:21)

Sending and the Spirit

Unless I go away, the Advocate will not come to you; but if I go, I will send him to you. (Jn 16:7)

The Advocate, the Holy Spirit, whom the Father will send in my name, will teach you all things and will remind you of everything I have said to you. (Jn 14:26)

Acknowledgments

FROM LANCE

Thanks to Brad for being smarter than me, putting up with my rants, talking me off ledges and being my dear friend.

Thanks to Rodger Peck for hearing the Lord, pushing me to move to Kansas City, and helping Sherri and me get started on the missional quest in what has become the city I love most. There is no way I can see it happening without you, my friend and brother.

Thanks to all the inspiring young men and women in Kansas City who have joined us in one way or another on this journey. There are so many of you, but no list would be complete without Josh and Trish Shepherd, Paul and Amanda Bartel, Jason and Nancy Phelps, Adam and Courtney Christensen, A. J. and Lindsay Vanderhorst, and Jay and Tiffany Sauser.

Thanks to my brothers in the Lord: Alan Hirsch and Michael Frost for teaching me forgotten ways and how to find the road to missional; Dan Southerland for being the living picture of servantship and a slice of Texas in KC; Kim Hammond for being perhaps the greatest example of a fivefold leader I have ever been around.

Thank to Dave Zimmerman. This is such a better book because of you.

To finish, I want to thank the entire Forge family. I will not name each of you for fear of leaving someone out. You are the tribe I spent my life looking for. I believe history will change because of you.

FROM BRAD

Thanks to Lance for pushing me to write. Without the constant nagging—I mean encouragement—this book would never have happened. I am glad to call you friend.

Thanks to Joshua, Caleb and Chloe for helping me to know what it means to love and be loved, and the more than fifty foster kids who have taught me what it means to be the real beneficiary of biblical hospitality. May God direct your steps daily.

Thanks to Dave Zimmerman for being such a great editor. It was wonderful to work with a publisher that not only understands the significance of the missional conversation for the American church but also deeply cares and appreciates what is involved.

Thanks to my ministry partners at both KNCSB and KCKBA for allowing me to serve as a church-planting catalyst in our region but also to serve Kansas City as a missionary that works with churches regardless of denominational affiliation. Thanks for being kingdom people.

Thanks to the Forge America national team, including Kim Hammond, Lance Ford, and Ryan and Laura Hairston. I look forward with great expectations to many years of mission together.

Finally, I want to thank Alan Hirsch for the intellectual rigor he has brought to the missional conversation as a whole, but also to my own personal edification. The best thing about Alan, however, is the way he models what it means to truly believe and live out the reality that "Jesus is Lord." Thanks for showing me what it looks like to be a man who really loves Jesus.

Notes

Chapter 1: The Starting Line

[1]Ferris L. McDaniel, "Mission in the Old Testament," in *Mission in the New Testament: An Evangelical Approach*, ed. William J. Larkin Jr. and Joel William (Maryknoll, NY: Orbis, 1998), pp. 12-15.

[2]Walter C. Kaiser Jr., *Mission in the Old Testament* (Grand Rapids: Baker, 2000), p. 11.

[3]R. Geoffrey Harris, *Mission in the Gospels* (London: Epworth, 2004), p. 227.

[4]Brad Brisco and Lance Ford, *Missional Essentials* (Kansas City, MO: House Studio, 2012).

[5]George Hunsberger, *The Church Between Gospel and Culture* (Grand Rapids: Eerdmans, 1996), p. 338.

[6]Ibid., p. 339.

[7]William R. McAlpine, *Sacred Space* (Eugene, OR: Wipf and Stock, 2011), p. 29.

[8]Alan Hirsch, *The Forgotten Ways* (Grand Rapids: Brazos, 2006), p. 133.

[9]Darrell L. Guder, *The Incarnation and the Church's Witness* (Eugene, OR: Wipf and Stock, 2004), p. xiii.

[10]Michael Frost, *Exiles* (Peabody, MA: Hendrickson, 2006), pp. 54-55; Brisco and Ford, *Missional Essentials*; Darrell Guder, *Incarnation and the Church's Witness*; R. Geoffrey Harris, *Misison in the Gospels*, pp. 228-32; Stephen Bevans, *Models of Contextual Theology* (Maryknoll, NY: Orbis, 1992); Ed Stetzer, "Why We Should Use the Phrase 'Incarnational Mission' (Part 1 of 3)," Ed Stetzer: The LifeWay Research Blog, June 20, 2011, www.edstetzer.com/2011/06/incarnational-mission-part-1.html.

[11]Alan Hirsch and Lance Ford, *Right Here, Right Now* (Grand Rapids: Baker, 2011), p. 249.

[12]Jon Huckins and Rob Yackley, *Thin Places* (Kansas City, MO: House Studio, 2012), p. 49.

[13]Frost, *Exiles*, p. 55.

[14]Brisco and Ford, *Missional Essentials*, p. 19.

[15]Harris, *Mission in the Gospels*, p. 229.

[16]Hirsch and Ford, *Right Here, Right Now*, p. 67.

[17]Harris, *Mission in the Gospels*, p. 227.

[18]Mark Van Steenwyk, "Incarnational Practices," *Next Wave*, http://outwardthinking.com/thenextwave/archives/issue82/index-64019.cfm.html.

Chapter 2: Stop and Go

[1]Stephen Bertman, *Hyperculture* (Santa Barbara, CA: Praeger, 1998), p. 2.

[2]Dallas Willard, *Renovation of the Heart: Putting on the Character of Christ* (Colorado Springs: NavPress, 2002), p. 29.

[3]James Wilhoit, *Spiritual Formation as if the Church Mattered: Growing in Christ Through Community* (Grand Rapids: Baker Academic, 2008), p. 7.

[4]Richard Rohr and John Feister, *Radical Grace: Daily Meditations* (Cincinnati: St. Anthony Messenger, 1993), p. 246.

[5]L. Paul Jensen, *Subversive Spirituality: Transforming Mission Through the Collapse of Space and Time* (Eugene, OR: Pickwick, 2009), p. 58.

[6]Henri Nouwen, Michael Christensen and Rebecca Laird, *Spiritual Formation* (San Francisco: HarperOne, 2010), p. 18.

[7]Ibid., p. 19.

[8]Keith Meyer, *Spiritual Rhythms in Community: Being Together in the Presence of God* (Downers Grove, IL: IVP Books, 2012), p. 15.

[9]Jessica Dickler, "$67 Billion in Vacation Days, Out the Window," CNNMoney, May 25, 2012, money.cnn.com/2011/05/25/pf/unused_vacation_days.

[10]Ibid.

[11]"Chick-fil-A's Closed-on-Sunday Policy," press release, S. Truett Cathy, www.truett cathy.com/pdfs/ClosedonSunday.pdf.

[12]Ibid.

[13]Sean Gladding, *The Story of God, the Story of Us: Getting Lost and Found in the Bible* (Downers Grove, IL: IVP Books, 2010), p. 25.

[14]Abraham Joshua Heschel, *The Sabbath: Its Meaning for Modern Man* (New York: Farrar, Straus and Young, 1951), p. 14.

[15]Dan B. Allender, *Sabbath* (Nashville: Thomas Nelson, 2009), p. 50.

[16]Jensen, *Subversive Spirituality*, p. 75

[17]Examples of fixed-hour prayer can be seen in the lives of Daniel (Dan 6:10) and David (Ps 55:17).

[18]Heschel, *Sabbath: Its Meaning*, p. 13.

[19]Peter Scazzero, *Emotionally Healthy Spirituality: Unleash a Revolution in Your Life in Christ* (Nashville: Integrity, 2006), p. 165.

[20]Phyllis Tickle, *The Divine Hours: Prayers for Autumn and Wintertime* (New York: Doubleday, 2000), p. xii.

[21]Nouwen et al., *Spiritual Formation*, p. 32.

Chapter 3: AD *30 All Over Again*

[1]Stuart Murray, *The Naked Anabaptist: The Bare Essentials of a Radical Faith* (Scottdale, PA: Herald Press, 2010), p. 52.

[2]Ibid.

[3]Stuart Murray, *Post-Christendom: Church and Mission in a Strange New World* (Carlisle, UK: Paternoster, 2004), p. 76.

[4]Reggie McNeal, "Reformed Church in America: One Thing: Reggie McNeal: It's AD 30 All Over Again," Vimeo video, 44:55, filmed at a gathering of Reformed Church in America leaders in San Antonio in 2008, vimeo.com/22618389.

[5]Wilbert R. Shenk, *Write The Vision: The Church Renewed* (Eugene, OR: Wipf and Stock, 1995), p. 3.

[6]Reggie McNeal, *The Present Future: Six Tough Questions for the Church* (San Francisco: Jossey-Bass, 2003), p. 47.

[7]Ed Stetzer, "Laypeople and the Mission of God, Part 1—Killing the Clergy-Laity Caste System," Ed Stetzer: The LifeWay Research Blog, July 17, 2012, www.edstetzer.com/2012/07/laypeople-and-the-mission-of-g.html.

[8]Chip Heath and Dan Heath, *Made to Stick: Why Some Ideas Survive and Others Die* (New York: Random House, 2007), p. 206.

Chapter 4: *Won't You Be My Neighbor?*

[1]Philip Langdon, *A Better Place to Live: Reshaping the American Suburb* (Amherst: University of Massachusetts Press, 1994), p. 19.

[2]Johannes Verkuyl, *Contemporary Missiology: An Introduction* (Grand Rapids: Eerdmans, 1975), pp. 387-92.

[3]Brad Brisco and Lance Ford, *Missional Essentials* (Kansas City, MO: House Studio, 2012), p. 67.

[4]Frank Charles Laubach, *Man of Prayer: Selected Writings of a World Missionary* (Syracuse, NY: Laubach Literacy International, 1990), p. 217.

[5]Brisco and Ford, *Missional Essentials*, p. 26.

[6]John Hayes, *Sub-merge: Living Deep in a Shallow World* (Ventura, CA: Regal, 2006), p. 181.

[7]John McKnight and Peter Block, *The Abundant Community: Awakening the Power of Families and Neighborhoods* (San Francisco: Berrett-Koehler, 2010), p. 70.

[8]Brisco and Ford, *Missional Essentials*, p. 68.

[9]McKnight and Block, *Abundant Community*, p. 70.

[10]Ibid.

[11]Michael Frost and Alan Hirsch, *The Shaping of Things to Come: Innovation and Mission for the 21st-Century Church* (Peabody, MA: Hendrickson, 2003), p. 25.

[12]Henri J. M. Nouwen, *Lifesigns: Intimacy, Fecundity, and Ecstasy in Christian Perspective* (Garden City, NY: Doubleday, 1986), p. 45.

[13]Not his real name.

[14]McKnight and Block, *Abundant Community*, p. 138.

Chapter 5: Home, Work and God's Mission

[1]J.R. Baxter Jr., 1946, Stamps-Baxter Music and Printing Co.

[2]Joe Purdue, "Sci-Fi Theology: Just Passin' Through," Red Letter Christians, October 28, 2011, www.redletterchristians.org/sci-fi-theology.

[3]Len Hjalmarson, "No Home Like Place: Seeking a Theology of Place," NextReformation: Leadership, Formation, Culture, May 2012, nextreformation.com/wp-content/uploads/2012/05/No-Home-Like-Place-Short.pdf.

[4]Wendell Berry, "How to Be a Poet," in *Given* (Berkeley, CA: Counterpoint, 2006), p. 18.

[5]Richard Soule, "This World Is Not My Home," FaithWriters: The Home for Christian Writers, June 19, 2005, www.faithwriters.com/article-details.php?id=29053.

[6]Christine Pohl, *Making Room: Recovering Hospitality as a Christian Tradition* (Grand Rapids: Eerdmans, 1999), p. 6.

[7]Brad Brisco and Lance Ford, *Missional Essentials* (Kansas City, MO: House Studio, 2012), p 72.

[8]Darrell L. Bock, "Luke 9:51-24:53," in *Baker Exegetical Commentary of the New Testament* (Grand Rapids: Baker, 1996), p. 1266.

[9]Christine Pohl, *Making Room: Recovering Hospitality as a Christian Tradition* (Grand Rapids: Eerdmans, 1999), p. 13.

[10]Elizabeth Newman, *Untamed Hospitality* (Grand Rapids: Brazos, 2007), p. 174.

[11]Pohl, *Making Room*, p. 6.

[12]Daniel Homan and Lonni Collins Pratt, *Radical Hospitality* (Brewster, MA: Paraclete, 2001), p. xxii.

[13]Alan and Deb Hirsch, *Untamed: Reactivating a Missional Form of Discipleship* (Grand Rapids: Baker, 2010), p. 166.

[14]Homan and Pratt, *Radical Hospitality*, p. 9.

[15]Ibid.

[16]John Stott, *Romans: God's Good News for the World* (Downers Grove, IL: InterVarsity Press, 1994), p. 332.

[17]Pohl, *Making Room*, p. 75.

[18]Ibid., p. 172.

[19]Ibid., p. 13.

[20]Kathryn Kleinhans, "The Work of a Christian: Vocation in Lutheran Perspective," *Word & World* 25, no. 4 (2005): 396.

[21]Ibid.

[22]Gene Edward Veith Jr., *God at Work* (Wheaton, IL: Crossway, 2002), p. 19.

[23]Christopher J. H. Wright, *The Mission of God's People* (Grand Rapids: Zondervan, 2010), p. 223.

[24]Veith, *God at Work*, p. 24.

Chapter 6: Where Everybody Knows Your Name

[1]Ray Oldenburg, *The Great Good Place* (New York: Paragon House, 1989), pp. 22-42.

[2]Ibid., p. 25.

[3]Ibid., p. 16.

[4]Ibid., p. 4.

[5]Robert D. Putnam and Lewis Feldstein, *Better Together: Restoring the American Community* (New York: Simon and Schuster, 2004); John McKnight and Peter Block, *The Abundant Community: Awakening the Power of Families and Neighborhoods* (San Francisco: Berrett-Koehler, 2010); Peter Block, *Community: The Structure of Belonging* (San Francisco: Berrett-Koehler, 2009).

[6]Robert D. Putnam, *Bowling Alone: The Collapse and Revival of American Community* (New York: Simon and Schuster, 2000), p. 103.

[7]Oldenburg, *Great Good Place*, p. 284.

[8]"The Origin of the Power of 10," PPS: Projects for Public Spaces, www.pps.org/reference/poweroften.

[9]Ibid.

[10]Oldenburg, *Great Good Place*, p. 296.

Chapter 7: Launching Pads

[1]Darrell L. Guder and Lois Barrett, *Missional Church: A Vision for the Sending of the Church in North America* (Grand Rapids: Eerdmans, 1998), p. 147.

[2]Michael Frost and Alan Hirsch, *The Shaping of Things to Come: Innovation and Mission for the 21st-Century Church* (Peabody, MA: Hendrickson, 2003), p. 76.

[3]Charles M. Olsen, *The Base Church: Creating Community Through Multiple Forms* (Atlanta: Forum House, 1973), p. 16.

[4]Justo Gonzáles, *Faith and Wealth* (New York: Harper & Row, 1990), p. 83.

[5]Norman Kraus, *The Community of the Spirit* (Scottdale, PA: Herald, 1993), p. 170.

[6]Alan Hirsch and Lance Ford, *Right Here, Right Now: Everyday Mission for Everyday People* (Grand Rapids: Baker Books, 2011), p. 187.

[7]Len Hjalmarson, "The Five-Fold Ministry and the Birth of New Movements," Next Reformation.com, nextreformation.com/wp-admin/leadership/five-fold.htm (accessed April 24, 2012).

[8]Lance Ford, *UnLeader: Reimagining Leadership . . . and Why We Must* (Kansas City, MO: Beacon Hill, 2012), p. 153.

[9]Barbara Kellerman, *Followership: How Followers Are Creating Change and Changing Leaders* (Boston: Harvard Business School Press, 2008), pp. 56-57.

[10]Lance Ford, *With Me: Relationship Essentials for A Discipleship Ethos*, ebook (Exponential, 2012).

[11]Brad Brisco and Lance Ford, *Missional Essentials: A Guide for Experiencing God's Mission in Your Life* (Kansas City, MO: House Studio, 2012), p. 89.

Chapter 8: Follow the Follower

[1]Alan Hirsch and Tim Catchim, *The Permanent Revolution: Apostolic Imagination and Practice for the 21st-Century Church* (San Francisco: Jossey-Bass, 2012), p. 21.

[2]Lance Ford, *UnLeader: Reimagining Leadership . . . and Why We Must* (Kansas City, MO: Beacon Hill, 2012), p. 20.

[3]Ed Stetzer, "7 Top Issues Church Planters Face, Issue #1: Leadership Development and Reproducing Culture," Ed Stetzer: The Lifeway Research Blog, January 12, 2011, www.edstetzer.com/2011/01/7-top-issues-church-planters-f.html.

[4]Ed Stetzer, "7 Issues Church Planters Face, Issue #4—System, Processes and Cultures," Ed Stetzer: The Lifeway Research Blog, January 26, 2011, www.edstetzer.com/2011/01/7-top-issues-planters-face-iss.html.

[5]Todd Wilson, quoted in Lance Ford, *Unleader* (Kansas City: NPH, 2012). His comments were originally posted at the Exponential website, www.exponential.org/2011/01/what-if/. They are, unfortunately, no longer archived there.

[6]Nannerl Keohane, "On Leadership," *Perspective on Politics* 3, no. 4 (December 2005): 715.

[7]Paul Stanley and J. Robert Clinton, *Connecting: The Mentoring Relationships You Need to Succeed* (Colorado Springs: NavPress, 1992), p. 18.

[8]Ibid., p. 38.

[9]Ibid.

Chapter 9: Have a Great Trip

[1]Albert Chen, "The Greatest Game Ever Pitched," *Sports Illustrated*, June 1, 2009, http://sportsillustrated.cnn.com/vault/article/magazine/MAG1155946/.

[2]Cathy Lynn Grossman, "As Protestants Decline, Those with No Religion Gain," *USA Today*, October 9, 2012, www.usatoday.com/story/news/nation/2012/10/08/nones-protestant-religion-pew/1618445.

[3]Charles Edward Van Engen, *God's Missionary People: Rethinking the Purpose of the Local Church* (Grand Rapids: Baker, 1991), p. 81.

[4]Alan Hirsch, *The Forgotten Ways: Reactivating the Missional Church* (Grand Rapids: Brazos, 2006), p. 182.

[5]Everett M. Rogers, *Diffusion of Innovations*, 3rd ed. (New York: Free Press, 1983), p. 11.

[6]Alan Hirsch and Dave Ferguson, *On the Verge: A Journey into the Apostolic Future of the Church* (Grand Rapids: Zondervan, 2011), p. 80.

[7]Ibid.

[8]Van Engen, *God's Missionary People*, p. 176.

Forge

How can God's people give witness to his kingdom in an increasingly post-Christian culture? How can the church recover its true mission in the face of a world in need? Forge America exists to help birth and nurture the missional church in America and beyond. Books published by InterVarsity Press that bear the Forge imprint will also serve that purpose.

Forge Books from InterVarsity Press

Creating a Missional Culture, by JR Woodward
Forge Guides for Missional Conversation (set of five), by Scott Nelson
The Missional Quest, by Lance Ford and Brad Brisco
More Than Enchanting, by Jo Saxton
The Story of God, the Story of Us, by Sean Gladding

For more information on Forge America, to apply for a Forge residency, or to find or start a Forge hub in your area, visit **www.forgeamerica.com**

For more information about Forge books from InterVarsity Press, including forthcoming releases, visit **www.ivpress.com/forge**